P̶ for *How to Get On with*
A̶

'One ... books on building good relationships in all aspects of your life.'
Linda Berens Ph.D.; author, Interaction Essentials; *creator of the Interaction Styles model; Director, Berens Institute*

'For l ... uthenticity is key and if you know and understand your own style your ... of being more effective as a leader and a human being will be greatly enha ... your interactions with others – this book is an essential guide.'
Mark Stewart, General Manager and HR Director, Airbus

'Lear ... out ourselves and how to relate optimally to others is a continuous proc ... practical and accessible manual, built around a proven model, will give ... nous help along that journey.'
Andrew Mayo, Professor of Human Capital Management, Middlesex University

'A "m ... d" book for every manager and for anyone working with people; with ... eful tools and frameworks to improve and manage interpersonal relat ...'
Fiona Colquhoun, Director and Mediator, CEDR - Centre for Effective Dispute Resolution

'If yo ... o feel motivated and energised, rather than frustrated and drained, this i ... ook for you – it's the ultimate guide to getting on with others.'
Ian Wrightson, Partner, UK Executive, Head of People and Culture, Mazars LLP

'This ... oth innovative and practical as it provides concrete yet comprehensive t ... lp each of us understand how our behaviour might unintentionally impa ... s well as gain insight into the positive intent that might be driving othe ... ur, when it is different to our own. It provides clear direction of how ... nally intelligent in the moment ... the book is delightful and well-written ... the link with Intention and Impact - very helpful!'
Susan Nash, Founder of the Type Academy

'A really practical book with lots of ideas and templates for real life situations at work and at home.'
Anne Whitaker, former Audit partner, EY

'Really interactive and practical with plenty of self-assessment opportunity...you will definitely learn something valuable and immediately applicable.'
Steve Jones, Operations Director, Laing O'Rourke

'Catherine has found the sweet spot between intellectual rigour and accessibility. The result is a great resource for OD practitioners and coaches to help clients discover and uncover aspects of interaction and self that will enable more effective ways of being, working and delivering in service of their work roles and teams.'

Sue Hills, Organisation Development
Manager, The King's Fund

How to Get On with Anyone

P

Pearson

At Pearson, we have a simple mission: to help people make more of their lives through learning.

We combine innovative learning technology with trusted content and educational expertise to provide engaging and effective learning experiences that serve people wherever and whenever they are learning.

From classroom to boardroom, our curriculum materials, digital learning tools and testing programmes help to educate millions of people worldwide – more than any other private enterprise.

Every day our work helps learning flourish, and wherever learning flourishes, so do people.

To learn more, please visit us at **www.pearson.com/uk**

How to Get On with Anyone

Gain the confidence and charisma to communicate with any personality type

Catherine Stothart

 Pearson

Harlow, England • London • New York • Boston • San Francisco • Toronto • Sydney
Dubai • Singapore • Hong Kong • Tokyo • Seoul • Taipei • New Delhi
Cape Town • São Paulo • Mexico City • Madrid • Amsterdam • Munich • Paris • Milan

Pearson Education Limited
KAO Two
KAO Park
Harlow CM17 9NA
United Kingdom
Tel: +44 (0)1279 623623
Web: www.pearson.com/uk

First edition published 2018 (print and electronic)

ISBN: 978-1-292-20786-5 (print)
　　　978-1-292-20787-2 (PDF)
　　　978-1-292-20788-9 (ePub)

British Library Cataloguing-in-Publication Data
A catalogue record for the print edition is available from the British Library

Library of Congress Cataloging-in-Publication Data
A catalog record for the print edition is available from the Library of Congress

10 9 8 7 6 5 4 3 2 1
22 21 20 19 18

Cover design by Two Associates

Print edition typeset in 9.5/13, Mundo Sans Pro by iEnergizer Aptara®, Ltd.
Printed by Ashford Colour Press Ltd, Gosport

NOTE THAT ANY PAGE CROSS REFERENCES REFER TO THE PRINT EDITION

Contents

CONTENTS

About the author

Catherine Stothart is a Leadership Coach and Team Facilitator and has run her own consultancy business since 2002, with clients including Airbus, Audi, the EEF, KCOM, Astra Zeneca and United Utilities. She previously held posts in Human Resource Management and Learning & Development in Ford Motor Company, Mercury Communications and ICL.

Catherine lived for several years in Cairo and Rio de Janeiro - these were life-enhancing experiences and really opened her eyes to human behaviour and cultural differences and her work has continued with the underlying themes of behavioural change and personal development ever since.

She has coached dozens of managers on topics such as influencing others, engaging their teams, building resilience and developing emotional intelligence. She coaches teams in high performance ways of working and has worked on many team and leadership programmes in major companies. She also works with teachers in local high schools in Cheshire, using personality type as a way of helping them understand themselves, their colleagues and their pupils. She has experience as a Chair of Governors and is a Trustee of the British Association of Psychological Type.

Catherine has a BA in English from the University of Oxford, an MSc in Organisational Behaviour from Birkbeck College, University of London, is a Fellow of the Chartered Institute of Personnel and Development, and has qualifications in coaching and psychometric testing.

Catherine has published articles in professional journals and this is her first book.

Acknowledgements

This book builds on and describes how to apply the Interaction Styles model, which was developed by Linda Berens in the US, and published in 2001. It is based on research she carried out over 20 years into personality type and temperament (Carl Jung[1], Keirsey and Bates[2]), and it also draws on work on observable behaviour patterns (such as Merrill and Reid's[3] social styles theory that was further developed by Bolton and Bolton[4], and the work of Marston[5], Geier and Downey[6]).

The model has four patterns of interaction, which Berens named In-Charge™, Chart-the-Course™, Get-things-Going™ and Behind-the-Scenes™. In this book I have given these four styles one-word names to make them more accessible to a wider audience, while retaining the integrity of her model. The names are: Mobiliser (for Berens' In-Charge), Navigator (for Berens' Chart-the-Course), Energiser (for Berens' Get-Things-Going) and Synthesiser (for Berens' Behind-the-Scenes). The descriptions of the styles closely follow those of Linda Berens and they are adapted with her permission.

I am very grateful to Linda Berens for supporting me in this work and giving me her invaluable advice on how to write about the styles. I am also full of admiration for the depth of her knowledge about personality types and her many years of work in this field. For more information about Interaction Styles, please see www.lindaberens.com

Particular thanks also go to:

- Susan Nash of the Type Academy, who has been so generous in sharing her time, expertise and resources with me.

- My editor, Eloise Cook, for her helpful guidance and suggestions, which made a positive difference to the book.

- Alison Smith, a good friend, for giving her time and her fantastic attention to detail, to reading drafts and suggesting improvements.

- Steve Temblett for advising me on how to write a publishing proposal.

- Georgia Parker, my coaching supervisor, for ideas and encouragement.

- Gill Hardy, Richard Moulds, Judy Done and other friends and colleagues, whose advice helped me along the way.

- David Hodgson, for passing on to me his experience of writing and publishing.

- Sue Blair, colleagues at the Type Academy and at the British Association for Psychological Type, for their interest and encouragement.

- All the leaders and teams to whom I have introduced Interaction Styles over the last seven years and from whom I have learned so much about personality and behaviour.

- Bill Stothart, my husband, for his unfailing love and support throughout our lives together and especially during the time it has taken to create this book.

Publisher's acknowledgements

The publisher would like to thank the following individuals and organisations for their kind permission to reproduce copyright material.

Photographs

123RF: Aleksangel 54; Getty Images: Bettmann 11; Shutterstock: Happy Art 12.

Illustrations

Adapted, with permissions, from Linda Berens, Interaction Essentials, 3 Proven Strategies to Remove Communication Barriers, 2015, 2011. Radiance House, Los Angeles, California

All other images © Pearson Education

Setting the scene

Only connect

E M Forster

We are social beings. For most of us, our relationships are the most important part of our lives. More than wealth or status, relationships with others are what give us meaning and a sense of purpose. There is convincing evidence that 'our relationships with other people matter, and matter more than anything else in the world'[7]. When our relationships are poor, we experience loneliness, distress and ill health. Good relationships are the basis for well-being and fulfilment.

But getting on well with other people at work and at home can be difficult – misunderstandings and conflicts arise, and we don't get the results we want. Worse than that, we may get results that we definitely don't want.

People have patterns of behaviour which they tend to repeat in a variety of situations and we describe this as their 'personality' or 'character', or 'the sort of person they are'. We sometimes talk of having a 'personality clash' with someone, which is shorthand for not getting on with them. It usually occurs because what they do or say, or what they think or feel, is different from us and we find their patterns of behaviour difficult to relate to. In other cases, we quickly feel rapport with people and easily get on well with them. This book will give you the awareness of why these differences occur and what you can do to get on better with all personality types.

The book is based on the four basic styles, known as Interaction Styles[8], which people tend to display when they communicate with others and it's about how to relate more successfully to other people, both at work and in our personal lives. It's a practical guide to how to adapt behaviour to connect with other people and get good outcomes for everyone. You will learn about the four styles and become aware of what might drive your words and actions and how to manage your impact on others. You will also be able to read other people's behaviours more accurately, appreciate what might be driving their behaviour and adapt what you say and do to build rapport and understanding with them.

I have been working with individuals and teams in business and education for 25 years and the most common problems they have relate to working with others. Interaction Styles is the best tool I have found to help them to gain self-insight and get on better with others. I've also personally found it immensely helpful in my own relationship with my husband and children. Often, when I introduce the styles when working as a coach in business, people see how they can apply it to their lives and relationships outside work, as much as in work. That is why I believe it is worth sharing it more widely, and why I have written this book.

A word of warning: People are very complex and no single model of human behaviour can account for all the variations between people. Our behaviour is influenced by our upbringing, education and the culture in which we live, as well as by our inborn personality preferences. Furthermore, in any situation we have choices about how we behave, and these are not pre-determined by our personality. But there are some recognisable patterns of behaviour that people share (while having many different individual characteristics), and knowing about the four Interaction Styles gives you both self-insight and options for how to interact with others to get better outcomes for everyone. I have found that people get it easily and can put it into practice quickly, with positive and constructive results.

How the book is set out

Part 1 sets out why the styles are important, what they are, and the typical strengths and potential pitfalls of each style.

- Chapter 1 sets the styles in the broader context of emotional intelligence and recent developments in neuroscience.

- Chapter 2 gives you the opportunity to assess your own style.

- Chapter 3 has an overview of the four styles – how people come across when they are in each style and what motivations might be driving their behaviour.

- Chapters 4–7 describe each of the four styles in detail, how to maxim-ise your strengths, recognise your emotional triggers and manage your response to conflict and stress.

Part 2 describes how to recognise the four styles in other people and gives tips on how to work and live with them.

- Chapter 8 focuses on awareness of others and how to pick up cues about their thoughts and feelings. It relates physical cues to the likely inner drives, beliefs and aims to give an appreciation of the usually positive intention behind behaviour.

- Chapters 9–12 are about living and working with people of each style – tips on what works well and potential conflicts and synergies with the other styles.

Part 3 covers specific applications of the styles in different situations and settings.

- Chapter 13 focuses on how to build rapport and trust, how to set positive outcomes and plan your communication to have the impact you intend.

- Chapter 14 is about how to flex your style to engage others and inspire their commitment, rather than just their compliance.

- Chapter 15 looks at sources of power and how to harness the talents of your style to enhance your charisma.

- Chapter 16 describes the strategies to build your self-esteem and self-confidence.

- Chapter 17 is about how to cope with pressure, manage stress and re-energise.

The Appendix includes handy reference and quick look-up tables.

How to use this book

If you want to dip into the book rather than reading it from cover to cover, start with Chapters 2 and 3 where you can do the self-assessment activities and get an overview of the four styles. Then you can read the chapter about your own preferred style (one of Chapters 4–7) and how to adapt to connect with others and behave in more emotionally intelligent ways. If you want tips on how to connect better with someone of one of the other styles, then read the chapter on living and working with that style (one of Chapters 9–12).

In Part 3 you will find practical tools and techniques for emotionally intelligent behaviour that apply to all styles – how to have positive impact and influence, how to engage others, how power affects communication, building your confidence and finally a chapter on maintaining your resilience and re-energising in today's hectic world.

Throughout the book there are activities and exercises for you to complete if you wish, so it can be used as a handbook for yourself or to use with others.

All the case studies are true, and all names have been changed.

Who this book is for

This book is for anyone who is interested in understanding themselves, understanding other people and building better relationships at work and at home. No prior knowledge is required, though there are plenty of references for anyone who wants to dig deeper into the theory and related models.

Reading this book will help you to:

- understand your own Interaction Style and how to manage your behaviour for positive impact and influence

- understand the Interaction Styles of others and how to get on better with them

- feel more confident and influential in your relationships, at work and at home

- discover how to flex your style to improve team work and get better results for everyone

- learn how to pick up cues from other people's behaviour so that you can successfully engage and inspire them

- feel motivated and energised when working with others instead of frustrated and drained

- reduce unnecessary conflicts and avoid misunderstandings when working with others.

I hope this book will help you to enjoy **all** your relationships to the full.

Part **1**

What's your style?

Chapter 1

Your brain and you

We see what is behind our eyes

Chinese proverb

Our conscious minds are tiny iceberg-tips on the dark ocean of unconscious

Oliver Burkeman[1]

Getting on with other people is one of life's biggest rewards and also one of its biggest challenges. We all know that we get on better with some people than others and that we can quickly build rapport with some people and take an instant dislike to others. While we can choose our friends, we can't choose our work colleagues, neighbours, family members, or the many people we meet in our daily lives. So anything which helps us get on better with others must be a good thing.

Everything we do or say has an impact on others, whether we intend it or not, and we communicate constantly. But we are not always aware of how we come across to others or the impact on them of our behaviour. Similarly, we are not always skilled at picking up cues from other people about the thoughts and feelings driving their behaviour and we don't always respond appropriately. If we can improve in these two areas, we will get on better with other people and have more satisfying relationships. What helps us to get on well with other people is to:

- know how we come across to others and be able to manage the impact we create

- pick up cues from them and adapt our behaviour to respond to them constructively.

In other words, we need to behave in more emotionally intelligent ways, with greater self-insight and better perception of others.

There are four styles that people typically fall into when they interact with others. Knowing about these four styles gives you the self-awareness, and the awareness of others, to behave with greater emotional intelligence and get on better with them.

The four Interaction Styles were researched and developed by Linda Berens[2] in the US and she named them In-Charge™, Chart-the-Course™, Get-things-Going™ and Behind-the-Scenes™. In this book I have given them the following one-word names:

- **MOBILISERS**: They push for action with results; they generally move and speak quickly and may be seen as straightforward and determined.

- **NAVIGATORS**: They push for a course of action; they generally move and speak in a deliberate manner and may be seen as serious and focused.

- **ENERGISERS**: They push for involvement; they generally move and speak enthusiastically and may be seen as expressive and engaging.

- **SYNTHESISERS**: They push for the best result; they generally move and speak patiently and may be seen as unassuming and approachable.

Before exploring the four styles, it is worth taking a little time to review:

- why it is important to be emotionally intelligent

- some findings from neuroscience that show that being emotionally intelligent is difficult

- how knowing about the four styles helps you to get on better with others.

Why emotional intelligence is important

Daniel Goleman[3] and others have shown that emotional intelligence is important for success in life. The key message of his book was that to live and work productively with other people, you need emotional intelligence (EQ) as much as IQ (intelligence quotient). For Goleman, EQ is being aware of your own emotions and being able to manage them, and being aware of the emotions of others and being able to build connections with them.

Goleman, a psychologist and science journalist, based his book on research carried out by various people, including Howard Gardner,[4] Paul Ekman[5] and Salovey and Mayer.[6] Ekman identified facial expressions for six emotions that are believed to be universally recognised across all human cultures – happiness, sadness, fear, surprise, anger and disgust.

A key part of emotional intelligence is empathy – the ability to detect the emotions of others and experience the same emotions yourself or at least to imagine what someone else is feeling.[7] Some politicians, like Bill Clinton and Barack Obama, are noted for showing empathy and this enabled them to connect with voters. In a presidential campaign debate in 1992, George H Bush notably failed to show empathy towards a woman who asked about how the downturn in the economy had personally affected him. He spoke about investing to get the economy going again, while Clinton walked up to the woman, looked her in the eye and talked about the people he personally knew who had been badly hit by the downturn. Afterwards, film of the event showed the woman nodding in response to Clinton's words, and showed that their facial expressions and tone of voice matched. They were in rapport and he was demonstrating empathy to her and, importantly for his election prospects, to the wider TV audience.

Empathy is a very basic characteristic, fundamental to all human relationships, and without empathy it is difficult to connect to other people. (There is evidence that other mammals also have empathy and are affected by emotions.)[8] Empathy and emotional intelligence are important for anyone who works with others, and especially for those in leadership positions, as 'leadership today is a deeply emotional role'.[9] Uwe Krueger,[10] the CEO of engineering company Atkins, describes emotional intelligence as the 'art of leadership': 'the emotional part is something that makes you authentic and that people expect from you in order to develop trust in you'.

And it goes further than creating trust. Neuroscientists agree that feelings and thinking are 'completely intertwined'[11] and that emotions (in ourselves or others) provide us with information that is necessary for decision-making. Without the emotional component of decision-making, our decisions would be worse. So, emotional intelligence (EQ) is not only 'nice to have' but is an essential part of working and living with others. Our ability to get along with other people in any context, outside work as well as in work, is aided by emotional intelligence and empathy.

Take a few moments to think about what emotional intelligence means to you. What examples do you have of emotionally intelligent behaviour? What behaviours would you class as good EQ? And what about emotionally UNintelligent behaviour? What would you class as poor EQ? Behaviour in this context is what you do, say, think or feel.

Some examples are given to start you off.

Your words and phrases to describe emotional intelligence
Being able to pick up on how someone else is feeling

Examples of emotionally intelligent behaviour	Examples of emotionally UNintelligent behaviour
Being able to respond calmly and assertively to someone who is angry	Giving negative feedback to someone in front of others

Notes

Recent findings in neuroscience

Behaving in an emotionally intelligent way depends on being aware of and able to manage the emotions driving our own behaviour. It is also about recognising the impact of our behaviour on others, being able to read their emotions and understand what might be driving their behaviour.

But this is not easy. Neuroscientists have shown that perception of the world around us is prone to distortion and error – our brains do not merely take in information from the world around us, but they actively create it.[12] We fill in the gaps and make inferences and assumptions that go beyond what we perceive in the external world. This gap-filling also applies to our perception of other people – we may read their words, voice tone and body language correctly, or we may get it wildly wrong. We put our own interpretations on what other people say and do, seeing their words and actions through the distortions of our own lenses.

We cannot know what it is like to be someone else. The Native American adage 'Don't judge a man until you have walked a mile in his shoes' is often quoted because it makes an important point. We make assumptions from other people's behaviour about their thoughts, feelings and motivations, but these can be incorrect. Most of us have had experiences where we got the wrong end of the stick or have been completely unaware of the undercurrents in a conversation. Similarly, we sometimes lack awareness of our own emotions, how they might be driving what we say and do and how that behaviour might be impacting others.

Neuroscientists are finding more and more evidence that our perceptions of the outer world, our memory of events, our perceptions of other people and even our self-perceptions are all subject to distortion and error and they believe that as much as 95% of brain activity is outside our conscious awareness.[13] Here are some examples.

Problems in sensory perception and memory

What we take in with our five senses from the external world is subject to processes in the brain which create the experience.[14] Our brains are not merely recording experiences, they are *creating* them. So even our basic senses of sight, hearing, taste, touch and smell cannot be trusted to tell us what is really there. The checkerboard illusion[15] and the McGurk[16] effect show how our sight and hearing can be distorted – look them up on YouTube. In both cases, the context influences the meaning we make from our perceptions. Similarly, the 'Pepsi paradox' shows how taste can be distorted by branding. People are more likely to choose Pepsi over Coca Cola in blind tastings but choose Coca Cola when they know what they are drinking. Their experience of the taste is influenced by unconscious factors, such as the packaging and image of the brand. Jonah Berger[17] suggests that 99.9% of our choices are influenced by forces of which we are unaware. Social influences shape many of our decisions in unconscious ways.

Memory is also influenced by factors outside the immediate sensory data. In an experiment carried out by Elizabeth Loftus,[18] researchers were able to convince adults that as children they had been lost in a shopping mall. They were told some basic information about the fictional event, and were asked how they had felt when lost. About 25% claimed to remember the incident. Not only were they able to talk about how they had felt, but when they were asked about the same (fictional) event again a week later, many of them added details as facts which had never happened and which they had not been told. People remember the general gist of an event but not the details and may add details over time that didn't happen, believing them to be true. Their memory is a memory of a thought or feeling, not of an event in the external world. Even ID parades are prone to error – 20% of the time people choose as the guilty subject someone who the police know for sure cannot possibly have committed the crime.[19]

Masses of sensory data bombard us continually, but we cannot possibly attend to all of it. Our unconscious continually processes information without our being consciously aware of it[20] and most of this data never comes into our conscious minds. It is believed we can only attend to around seven items of the many millions of bits of data around us at a time – and our brains find ways of selecting relevant information. Sometimes a change occurs which causes things, that were previously unnoticed, to come into our conscious awareness. Several years ago, I wanted to change my car and became interested in a particular model that I had never previously noticed. Suddenly, the roads seemed to be full of cars like the one I was interested in. They had been there all the time, but I had never noticed them. Most people have had similar experiences. When we are sensitised to something, we notice it while ignoring other aspects. Try the illusion of the moonwalking bear on YouTube.

Sometimes, our brains record an event that only comes into consciousness later – if relevant. I once had my purse pickpocketed from my handbag. I discovered the loss only when I got home but I had an instant recall of when it had happened and who had done it, though at the time I had not consciously been aware of the theft. Most of us have had similar examples of realising the significance of an event only afterwards, when something causes it to come into conscious awareness.

Problems in perception of other people

The examples above show that what we perceive through our five senses, and our memory of events, can be distorted and much of our brain activity is outside our conscious awareness. If our perceptions of basic objects, like a chess board or a can of coke, can be inaccurate, then think how much more potential for error and distortion there is in our perceptions of other people, with all their additional complexities of language and behaviour.

Neuroscientists believe that much of our perception of other people happens unconsciously.[21] We automatically infer mental states from face, voice tone and body language. Our inferences may be correct or incorrect and as this happens unconsciously, it is next to impossible to know which is which. Furthermore, when we feel threatened, the unconscious takes over and the more primitive parts of the brain react with the fight or flight response. Steve Peters calls this instinctive reaction 'the inner chimp'[22] – the chimp acts before our conscious mind can decide on a more emotionally intelligent reaction.

When communicating with other people, we pay attention not just to what they say, but also to the way that they say it, their facial expression and tone of voice. Alfred Mehrabian's[23] research is often misquoted, but in essence, his study of the communication of emotion showed that when there is a contradiction between the words used and the tone of voice and facial expression, we pay more attention and trust the message conveyed by the tone of voice and facial expression than to the message of the words themselves. Note that this research specifically covered communication of *emotion*, not all communication.

Faces and eyes are especially important as our instinctive reactions to events are often revealed in our facial expressions. When we watch a film, we react emotionally and instinctively to the events on the screen. This is shown in our facial expressions, even though we are not communicating with anyone – it happens outside our conscious control. When talking to others, our brain pays attention to the minute muscle changes in their expressions and it is believed that this is one way we send and receive signals about our emotions. We unconsciously mirror these expressions and as a result, our brains experience and recognise the emotion our colleague is experiencing.

One rather scary consequence of this is that people who have had Botox injections in their face are less able to move their facial muscles and therefore less able to experience and understand the emotions of the people with whom they interact.[24]

There are several well-known examples of the impact of face and posture on people's interpretations of events. Researchers studied the impact of visual impression in the presidential debates between Nixon and Kennedy in 1960. During the TV debates, Nixon looked pale, haggard and sweaty, while Kennedy appeared suntanned and healthy. People who heard the debate on the radio rated Nixon as most effective, while those who saw the debate on TV said Kennedy did better.

Tone of voice has been shown to have an impact on the inferences that people make about the competence of the speakers. One set of experiments[25] used a computer to teach a topic, with either a female voice or male voice. When the topic was love and relationships, the students rated the female-voiced computer as having a more sophisticated knowledge of the topic than the male-voiced computer, even though the words spoken were the same. On gender-neutral topics, both were rated equally for competence. When a forceful male voice was used, it was rated as more 'likeable' than a forceful female voice, even when speaking exactly the same words.

It appears that when we observe other people, our brains do not merely record the observations, but *create* them. Our brains fill in the gaps and supply information that does not directly come from the raw sensory data. We make inferences about other people based on our perceptions of their facial expression, tone of voice, body language, and possibly other factors of which we are not even aware. Our inferences may be right or wrong and often we can only guess what other people are thinking and feeling. Consequently, our impressions and decisions about other people may not be accurate. We may be influenced by irrelevant attributes or superficial qualities and make erroneous decisions as a result.

Our judgements of other people are often made on guesswork and assumptions rather than hard evidence, and this can lead to bad decisions being made. Neville Chamberlain[26] wrote to his sister in 1938 after meeting Hitler that 'in spite of the hardness and ruthlessness I thought I saw in his face, I got the impression that here was a man who could be relied upon when he had given his word'.

Research into job interviews[27] has consistently shown that we make judgements about people as soon as they walk through the door, though if we give them a fair chance to answer the questions, we often find our initial impressions disproved. Despite all this evidence, we are often very confident in our ability to judge other people – whether on their competence, their honesty, or indeed if we like them.

Reflect on a recent interaction with someone.

What messages did you pick up from their facial expression and tone of voice? How accurate were those messages? How do you know?

Problems in knowing ourselves

Although we may agree that it is difficult to understand other people, most of us believe we have a pretty good understanding of ourselves. However, there is plenty of evidence from neuroscience that suggests we don't know ourselves nearly as well as we might think. The Milgram experiments (in which people thought they were giving electric shocks to others, some strong enough to kill) are a good example of this. Most of us believe that we would disobey the instructions of the authority figure to administer the shocks, yet the evidence of the experiments suggests that most of us would obey.

The planning fallacy is another example of our ignorance about ourselves. Despite experience that we consistently under-estimate how long it will take to carry out a task, we continue to underestimate. This applies as much to major construction projects like the Channel Tunnel, the Scottish Parliament and the London Olympics, as to our personal activities, clearing out the garage, digging the garden or sorting out our photos.

A particularly striking example of our inability to fully know our own minds is an experiment[28] in which people were shown pictures of two people and asked to choose which one they found more attractive. The pictures were then removed, and the participant was presented with one picture, and asked to explain why they chose it. Sometimes the picture was the one they had chosen, while in other cases they were shown the picture they had not chosen. Nevertheless, most people came up with an explanation of why they had chosen it, even when they hadn't. 'We often do not know what we like or why we like what we do. Our preferences are riddled with unconscious biases, easily swayed by contextual and social influences.'[29]

How the styles help

We know that our perceptions of the world around us and of other people can be incorrect, and that reading other people is prone to distortion and error. We often misinterpret what other people mean and react in ways that lead to further misunderstandings, confusion and even conflict. Similarly, we know that much goes on in our brains outside our conscious awareness and that even our understanding of our own motivations and behaviours can be limited. So how can an understanding of the styles help?

Knowing about the styles helps us interpret our own and other people's behaviour, and provides a guide for how to behave in more emotionally intelligent ways. Importantly, it connects the inner and outer worlds and the inner motivation to the outer behaviour. It helps us get in touch with ourselves and manage the emotions driving our own behaviour, as well as read the energy of other people and appreciate what might be driving their behaviour. It helps us fill in the gaps with something better than guesswork so that we can shift our communications and energy to connect better with them.

The diagram below shows the key components of emotional intelligence – self-awareness and being able to manage your own emotions, and awareness of others and being able to manage relationships with them. Your natural style is like a pivot around which you can shift your energy and communications and flex your approach to behave with greater emotional intelligence and build better relationships.

The EQ Equilibrium

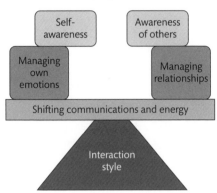

EQ, like IQ, may come more naturally to some people than others, but emotionally intelligent behaviours and attitudes can be developed. Emotional intelligence is 'the practice of managing one's personality'[30] – it is something that you do, rather than something that you have. The styles provide practical insights for behaving in an emotionally intelligent way in the moment, so that you can get on better with other people. The next chapter outlines the four styles.

Chapter 2

What are the styles and what's your style?

O, wad some Power the giftie gie us
To see oursels as others see us!

Robbie Burns

What are the styles?

People have natural patterns of behaviour that reflect their personality. We describe people as outgoing, reserved, serious, chatty, thoughtful, intense, friendly, argumentative, enthusiastic, bossy and so on. When we communicate with other people, we instinctively pick up cues from the way they move, how they speak, and the expressions on their faces. We interpret these cues and create an impression of the person, their personality and of their current state of mind, which may or may not be accurate, as we saw in the last chapter.

Similarly, they make assumptions about us based on how we come across to them. Although we have many individual and unique characteristics, we have a natural inclination to behave in certain ways and there are four fundamental patterns that we typically display when interacting with others. These patterns of behaviour are the four styles. We have a natural preference for one of these styles, but we can move into the other styles when the situation requires it.

The styles are patterns of physical and verbal behaviour, displayed when interacting with others, linked to underlying inner drives, beliefs, aims and talents.

The patterns of behaviour are the combination of physical energy (shown in our movement, gestures, and pace and tone of voice) with our inner beliefs and drives. These give a certain type of momentum to our behaviour and the pattern we display gives an impression of ourselves to others and has an impact on them.

The four styles affect how we interact with others and how we influence them, often non-verbally and sometimes without conscious intention. While the appearance of each style is visible, the underlying core belief, drive and aim are usually not obvious to others and sometimes not even known to ourselves. When we know what is driving our own behaviour, we are better able to manage our impact on others, and when we sense what might be driving other people's behaviour, we are able to respond more constructively.

How can the styles help me?

Each style has specific patterns of communication and decision-making that have an impact on interactions with others:

- Knowing your own natural style helps you make conscious choices about your behaviour in different situations.

- Understanding other people's style helps you build rapport with them and engage and influence them.

- Knowing your style helps you manage your stress points when interacting with others.

> **By linking external behaviours to likely inner drives, our judgements of others can be more accurate and our responses more appropriate.**

Knowing about the styles is helpful in almost any situation where you are interacting with other people, both at work and in your life outside work.

Josh, the manager of a business, used the styles as a guide to communicating with the members of his management team. He told me: 'There is more tolerance in management meetings now and when some of the team need more detail about plans, we understand why, whereas previously we'd just be thinking that we'd already gone over that. I have changed the way in which I present tasks to different team members, and I've noticed that the team are getting things done more quickly.'

Josh used his knowledge of the different communication styles of his team to adapt his approach, with successful results.

Here are some important points to bear in mind about the styles:

- They do not describe the whole of your personality – people are far more complex than can be described in one model.

- They are specifically about **how we interact** with others, not about other aspects of your personality.

- How we behave in any situation is influenced by our upbringing, education, experiences and the culture in which we live, as well as by our personality.

- They are highly situational. While we have a natural tendency to behave in certain ways, we can flex our style depending on the needs of the situation. Indeed, we often flex our behaviour unconsciously as a natural response to a situation.

> *Susie consciously chose to adopt a particular style, different from her natural style, when coaching juniors at badminton. This enabled her to project the authority she needed to maintain control of a large group of energetic teens and pre-teens. This style worked successfully for her and she built a reputation as an effective sports coach. However, she knew that the effort of adopting this style drained her energy, so after coaching sessions, she gave herself time for some of her favourite activities, to re-energise.*

The four styles

Here are some of the physical energies and inner beliefs and drives of the four styles, together with the names I use. Bear in mind that a single word cannot reflect the full meaning of each style.

NAVIGATOR	SYNTHESISER
Believe it's worth the **effort** to think ahead to reach the goal	Believe it's worth the **time** it takes to integrate and reconcile many inputs
Display **focused** energy – calm and methodical	Display **approachable** energy – open and patient
Make **deliberate** decisions to get the **desired** result	Make **consultative** decisions to get the **best result** possible
Can be perceived by others to be formal and serious	Can be perceived by others to be unassuming and modest

MOBILISER	ENERGISER
Believe it's worth the **risk** to go ahead and act or decide	Believe it's worth the **energy** spent to involve everyone and get them to want to...
Display **determined** energy – quick-moving and energetic	Display **engaging** energy – involving and expressive
Make **quick** decisions to get an **achievable** result	Make **collaborative** decisions to get an **embraced** result
Can be perceived by others to be straightforward and direct	Can be perceived by others to be persuasive and enthusiastic

Adapted from Linda Berens and Susan Nash[1]

On first sight, these approaches may seem similar, but in fact the four approaches reflect very different aims and motivations as follows:

- People with the energiser style, who want an 'embraced' result, are driven to involve others.

- People with the synthesiser style, who want 'the best possible' result, are driven to consult and gather information.

- People with the navigator style, who want a 'desired' result, are driven to identify a course of action.

- People with the mobiliser style, who want an 'achievable' result, are driven to get things accomplished.

Think about how you make decisions. Which of the four statements above best represents what is driving your behaviour?

- Do you want to get a quick and 'good enough' result (mobiliser style)?

- Do you want people to be engaged and 'bought into' the result (energiser style)?

- Do you want to deliberate over the decision and think through how the result will be achieved (navigator style)?

- Or do you want to make sure it is the best possible result and takes into account all relevant factors and opinions (synthesiser style)?

You might say you want to do all those things, and in an ideal world that is true. However, we naturally prioritise one style of decision-making over the others.

It can be helpful to think about how you make decisions outside work. My natural style is synthesiser, and I have a strong drive to get the best result possible. One way this comes out is when I am deciding which route to take when travelling to a new destination. I like to get information on all the possible routes, then weigh up the pros and cons of each (time, distance, likely hold-ups, scenery and coffee stops). I don't trust my satnav to take all these factors into account. If I follow my satnav then later discover that it was not the most effective route, I feel mortified. The fact that this is an extreme reaction to a trivial problem is an indication that getting the best result is a core driver for me.

By contrast, someone with the mobiliser style would make a quick decision on which route to take and would get on with it, without worrying about whether it was the best route. Indeed, they would wonder why I would bother to spend so much time and effort on an unimportant decision.

The table showing the four styles above refers to different types of energy, and even though we have a natural energy we will all have experienced the other energies too, when the situation requires it, as follows:

- 'Focused' energy (Navigator) is similar to the energy we experience when revising for or sitting an exam.

- 'Determined' energy (Mobiliser) is similar to the energy we experience when in a hurry to get somewhere.

- 'Engaging' energy (Energiser) is similar to the energy we experience when hosting a party.

- 'Approachable' energy (Synthesiser) is similar to the energy we experience when observing something and taking it all in.

The table also refers to how people in each style tend to move physically and how others may perceive their communication style. It is often easier to recognise these behaviours in other people than in ourselves, so you may find it useful to ask for feedback from others to help you assess your own style. And there are times when the situation demands that you move in a particular way. Although I naturally have the synthesiser style, when I am in a hurry or need to give direction to others my energy will appear to be the mobiliser style.

> **Which style do you think might fit you most naturally? If you are uncertain, you may find it helpful to eliminate the styles that do not come most naturally to you.**

Here are some key points to consider:

- The four patterns of energy and outward behaviour are correlated with inner drives, aims, beliefs and talents that influence how we engage with others to meet our needs.

- The four styles affect how we make decisions and how we communicate with others.

- The four styles are distinguished by three pairs of separate preferences that underlie the overall patterns (though the styles are more than the sum of these parts).

These underlying preferences give us insights into which overall pattern might fit best and they are:

- the role we take in setting pace and tone in an interaction – either by initiating communication or responding to it

- the way we aim to influence others – either by using directing or informing communication (tell or suggest)

- where we focus our attention when interacting – either on control over the outcome, or on the process for moving forward.

When interacting with others, the external energy people display gives an insight into their *internal state at that time* and we can use this indication to adapt our own behaviour to fit the circumstances.

This linking of body and mind, inner and outer worlds is what makes the styles such a powerful and helpful framework for understanding human behaviour.

One way to get an indication of your own style is by exploring the preferences that underlie the overall patterns. The sections that follow contain activities to help you consider where you naturally sit on the preferences which underlie the whole patterns.

Role polarities – the role we take in setting pace and tone

In setting the pace and tone of an interaction, people usually have a preference either for an initiating role, where they tend to speak or act first, or a responding role, where they tend to wait for the other person to make the first move. (Note that initiating a communication is not the same as having initiative).

Think about what might be your natural preference rather than the behaviour you might adopt due to your formal role or the situation. For example, if you are in sales, you will probably show initiating behaviours, even though your natural preference might be for responding. If you are a junior person meeting someone more senior, you might show responding behaviour, even though your natural preference might be for initiating.

The questionnaire below will help you think about how you naturally behave in interactions, while recognising that in specific situations you may choose to behave differently.

For each pair of items, tick the one that applies to you more than the other. Think about how you are in general, both in and outside work, rather than how you are forced to behave by circumstances.

	I prefer to think things through before speaking	I will often think things out by talking them through	
	I do not have a high need to meet regularly with others	I enjoy meeting other people and often seek social gatherings	

	I like to concentrate on a few tasks at a time	I enjoy a variety of tasks and activities	
	I dislike unanticipated interruptions	I am stimulated by unanticipated interruptions	
	When speaking publicly, I like to prepare in depth	When speaking publicly, I will often talk impromptu	
	I may be relatively quiet at meetings	I am likely to say a lot at meetings	
	I am generally likely to consider things before acting	I am more likely to act before deliberating	

Count up the ticks on each side, and whichever has the greatest number is likely to be your natural preference, though you can adapt your behaviour depending on the circumstances.

The left-hand side relates to the 'Responding' preference, while the right-hand side relates to the 'Initiating' preference.

Make a note here of which one seems to be your preference: _____

It is worth noting that in Western culture we may be socialised towards demonstrating initiating behaviours, so it can be difficult to assess your natural preference.

The table below shows the typical characteristics of the two preferences.

RESPONDING	INITIATING
Tend to wait for others to make the first contact	Tend to reach out to initiate contact
Energy moves inside first then to the outer world	Energy moves outside first then to the inner world

(Continued)

Quiet, slower pace, patient – sustained use of time	Animated, faster pace, active – quick use of time
Tend to reflect first then speak or act	Tend to speak and act then reflect
Contained gestures	Expressive gestures
Pressured by a fast pace	Impatient with slow pace
May be seen as withholding	May be seen as intrusive

Adapted from Linda Berens and Susan Nash

Typical behaviours of responding and initiating

In meetings at work when something comes up for discussion, do you find that other people seem to give their opinions quickly, while you are still thinking about it (responding)? Or are you one of the first to speak when a topic comes up for discussion (initiating)?

When you are out with a group of friends do you find that just as you are about to say something, the others move on to another topic (responding)? Or are you one of those leading the conversation (initiating)? Do you expect people to take it in turns to speak (responding), or are you comfortable with people speaking over each other (initiating)?

Do you like a quiet environment for concentration (responding), or do you prefer a busy environment for stimulation (initiating)?

These options are not totally either/or as we display a mixture of these behaviours, depending on the circumstances. However, most of us instinctively know in general where our comfort zone lies.

Based on your preference for either initiating or responding, consider the questions below and add your own comments. Some examples are given to start you off.

What might be the benefits of this preference for someone in your role (at home or work)?

If initiating, it might get the conversation going/If responding it might be good at listening

What might be the pitfalls for someone in your role?

If initiating it might not give space for other people to think and contribute/If responding it might be difficult to get your ideas heard

What do you admire most about the other preference?

Initiating – their energy and enthusiasm/Responding – their ability to think deeply

What do you appreciate least about the other preference?

Initiating – can be overpowering/Responding – can appear uninterested

These are some of the benefits and pitfalls of these preferences.

	Benefits	Potential pitfalls
Responding preference	They listen They take more time They help others slow down They have a calming influence They think things through	They may appear slow They may not get into the conversation They may appear reluctant to give input They may withdraw from or avoid conflict
Initiating preference	They kick things off They have a fast pace They communicate their thoughts They have an energising influence They give a quick response	They may rush through things They may dominate the conversation They may not listen to others They may increase their energy when dealing with conflict

Extraversion and introversion

The initiating-responding dimension is similar to the extraversion-introversion preference which you may be familiar with from other personality models. Here, though, it is a narrower concept and refers primarily to behaviour and energy during interactions, with the energy of the responding preference being more internally focused while the energy of the initiating preference is more externally focused. The distinction between using time quickly or using time in a more sustained manner is a key differentiator of initiating and responding. So, initiating behaviour might show in being the first to speak, in freely giving opinions, moving the conversation on, while responding behaviour might show in listening to others, thinking it through and spending time on each point.

The preference for initiating or responding does not necessarily relate to quantity of contribution to a conversation. People with the responding (or introversion) preference may have plenty to say when the topic of conversation interests them. Similarly, people with the initiating (extraversion) preference may remain silent when the topic is not relevant to them.

In Western culture, extraversion as a personality characteristic is generally valued more highly than introversion. In the Big 5 personality model,[2] introversion is regarded simply as an absence of extraversion, rather than as something that has positive elements in its own right. In popular culture, we may associate extraversion with positive descriptors such as being outgoing and fun, while introversion is sometimes associated with negative descriptors such as being reserved and a loner; however, extraversion could also imply arrogant and domineering while introversion could imply thoughtful and considerate.

In reality, most of us show a mixture of both introverting behaviours (a focus on our own thoughts and feelings) and extraverting behaviours (a focus on the external world), though the balance between them might vary. Nobody could be totally either one or the other – if they were, they would be either a hermit or a perpetual party-goer. Neither is in itself good or bad – the important thing is to know yourself so you can manage your energy and how much interaction you have with others and manage how you come across to others. Susan Cain[3] makes a convincing case for valuing the introversion preference and gives plenty of examples of people with this preference who have made significant contributions in their fields.

Problems can arise when people are different on this polarity – they see the negative sides of the other behaviour and don't feel appreciated for their own positive attributes. The following descriptions, from workshop discussions among groups of teachers, are their perceptions of initiating and responding behaviours. They illustrate how we may perceive our opposites negatively and also what we want our opposites to appreciate about us.

How people with the responding preference see people with the initiating preference:

- Confident, loud, lively, controlling, better

- Able to deal with confrontation

- Exhausting, noisy, pushy, nosey

- Full of energy and beans

- Lack inhibition, don't worry about what people think, fearless

- Big personality, in the zone

How people with the initiating preference see people with the responding preference:

- Quiet, slow, considered, contained

- Self-sufficient – we need you, but you don't appear to need us

- Good listeners, reflective, thoughtful

- Difficult to get to know in a group, reserved, not easy to talk to

- Calm exterior

- Communicating when there is a purpose

What those with the responding preference want those with the initiating preference to appreciate about them:

- We don't like being the centre of attention.

- We are happy with our own space and don't need constant interaction.

- We may appear standoffish, but we are friendly and approachable.

- We may be quiet, but we do have opinions and ideas.

- If we choose to say something it is really important to us and we have thought about it.

- Sometimes when we are quiet, we are just thinking and we are not anxious or upset.

What those with the initiating preference want those with the responding preference to appreciate about them:

- We need responses and feedback.

- We look for opportunities to connect with people.

- We have drive and energy.

- We sometimes speak without thinking and we need to talk things through.

- We are social animals, we enjoy company and take pleasure in conversation.

- Silence is uncomfortable and unsettling – what are you thinking?

What is striking about the statements from the two groups of teachers is how much the teachers with the initiating preference *need* interaction with other people, while teachers with the responding preference *need* time alone. By sharing their perceptions of each other, they were able to appreciate the needs of their opposites and adapt their behaviour. People with the initiating preference gave their colleagues more time to think about a topic in advance and listened to them when they had something to say. They learned that talking over them or interrupting caused them to stop communicating. People with the responding preference gave their colleagues the opportunity to talk things out – they learned that this helped them to work out their thoughts.

As well as communicating better with colleagues, being aware of the difference between responding and initiating helped this group of teachers to use a variety of different learning strategies to appeal to pupils with both preferences. They allowed some individual work as well as group work, and built in some quiet time as well as discussion time during lessons.

In the general population, preferences for introversion and extraversion are probably split roughly 50/50.[4] This means that we all know, work and live with people who are different from ourselves in relation to this preference. It is the preference that we most easily identify in other people and most likely will determine whether we like them or not. It is often easier to build rapport and understanding with people who are like us, but the effort put in to build relationships with people who are different from us is often repaid by the benefits of more effective team-working and decision-making in the workplace, and a greater variety of relationships at home.

In our personal lives, an understanding of this difference enables us to manage our expectations of others. For example, someone with the initiating preference might want to spend more time socialising than their partner with the responding preference.

> In a family, the parents and older teenager shared the responding preference while the younger teenager had the initiating preference. The younger son was talkative, had lots of friends, and he often invited friends back after school and liked to be out with them at weekends. His father frequently told his son to 'think before you speak' and not to 'talk all the time', but learning about the styles helped the father to appreciate that it was natural for his son to communicate his thoughts as soon as they occurred to him.
>
> In another family, the parents both had the initiating preference and were very worried about their quiet child, who preferred to go to her room when she came home from school and read a book, rather than be out at after-school activities. After communicating all day long with her teachers and other pupils, she needed time alone. Her parents learned not to worry about this or to nag her to participate in too many activities and they had a much happier relationship, where they no longer made her feel that there was something wrong with her.

Now that you have read about the benefits and potential pitfalls of responding and initiating, reflect again on your own preference. When does it come out?

In what situations, with whom, when?

(Continued)

What is the impact on achieving the outcome you want?

What is the impact on your relationship with the other person?

What opportunities to connect with others might be missed due to your preference?

If you behaved in line with the opposite preference, what would you do and say in a specific situation?

What result might you get?

Stephen, an active, energetic and outgoing manager of a car dealership, found it difficult to work with Ali, who was quiet, did not say much at meetings, and did not appear enthusiastic about his work and the business. Stephen had got to the point where he felt that Ali was not pulling his weight. After some coaching on the styles, Stephen learned that the main difficulty boiled down to a difference in style – while he expected people to express their enthusiasm, Ali was much more contained and felt overpowered by Stephen's energy. Stephen experimented with a more low-key, patient approach, and found that Ali had a lot to contribute when he was given the space and opportunity.

While there is potential for difficulties between people with opposite preferences, problems can also arise when people have the same preference: two people with the initiating preference may not listen to each other, while people with the responding preference may not communicate.

The point is to be aware of how your natural preference impacts your behaviour and whether that is effective for you in all situations.

If you are hoping to meet new people and make new friends, you may need to 'tune up' if you have the responding preference, by making an effort to initiate conversation and contribute to discussions, so that people can get to know you. If you are in the same situation with the initiating preference, you may need to 'tune down' your contributions to discussion, by asking questions and listening so that people feel you are interested in them.

Preferences for responding and initiating are especially relevant for managing meetings. If your team members mainly have initiating preferences, there will be a lot of talk and discussion during the meeting, whereas if they mainly have responding preferences, you may find it difficult to get people to speak up and articulate their thoughts. If one or two people are in the minority, they are likely to find the meetings unproductive – a minority of initiating people will feel frustrated by the lack of discussion, while a minority of responding people will feel frustrated by too much discussion. It's worth thinking about what you can do – before, after or during the meeting – to ensure that everyone has an appropriate opportunity to contribute.

It is also helpful to know which *in general* is the more productive environment for you, and to do what you can to influence it. If you have the responding preference and work in a busy, noisy office, you may be able to get some time to yourself during breaks. Conversely, if you have the initiating preference and work in a quiet place like a library, you may want to find people to interact with at break times.

When the working environment does not completely fit your preference, you might need to find some balance by compensating in your home life. Someone with the responding preference who works in a busy office with lots of interaction with others might need to have more time alone to recover and renew their energy when at home, before they are ready to chat to their partner. Someone with the initiating preference who works in a job where there is little interaction with others might need to be involved in many activities with other people outside work.

> **How can you ensure you meet your needs for interaction or time alone?**

Communication polarities – the way we aim to influence others

When interacting with others to make decisions or get things done, people tend to naturally have either a directing or an informing style of communication. People with a directing style have a task and time focus and tend to be comfortable telling others what to do, while people with an informing style have a focus on getting buy-in and prefer to give information, leaving the choice of whether or how to act to the other person. Again, the situation will influence which style is actually used, but nevertheless, we usually have a preferred style.

In a work situation, when there is a problem to resolve, someone with a directing style might give direction: 'I think what we need to do is...', or 'You should do it this way...', while a person with an informing style might want to give and receive input: 'There are lots of aspects to consider', or 'What does everyone think?'

At home, when noticing that the grass has grown too long, someone with the directing preference might say: 'Please cut the grass' while someone with the informing preference might say: 'The grass needs to be cut.'

Here are some more examples:

Directing	Informing
Please close the door	The door is still open
Who has moved the coffee?	Where's the coffee gone?
Please tidy your room	It would help me if you could tidy your room
Are you ready yet?	How long will it be before you are ready?
Can I use the computer now please?	How much longer are you going to be on the computer?

We even ask questions differently, depending on our preference. In the final question above, the informing preference is seeking information to help decide what to do next, while the directing preference is making a direct, unambiguous request.

For each pair of items below, tick the one that applies to you more than the other. Think about how you are in general, both in and outside work, rather than how you are forced to behave by circumstances. Most people will have a mixture of directing and informing behaviours, but your responses can help you decide which preference comes most naturally to you.

	I put my ideas forward clearly	I tend to explore alternatives with people before deciding	
	I tend to tell people what to do to motivate them	I tend to make suggestions to others to motivate them	
	When someone says something I disagree with, I usually tell them so	I tend to avoid expressing disagreement unless it is really necessary	
	I usually have a course of action in mind before speaking to others for input	I like to discuss all the options before deciding what to do	
	I'd rather tell people what to do so they know what's expected	I'd rather give people options than tell them what they should do	
	My priority is to get the task done on time	I know that involving others will result in something better	
	I decide what needs to be done and I suggest to others what to do and how to do it	I explain the situation, ask for ideas and gather information, then I/we decide what needs to be done	

(Continued)

Count up the ticks on each side, and whichever has the greatest number may be your natural preference, though you can of course adapt your behaviour depending on the circumstances.

The left-hand side relates to the 'directing' preference, while the right-hand side relates to the 'informing' preference.

The table below shows the typical characteristics of the two preferences when communicating.

DIRECTING	INFORMING
Focus on task and time – their unconscious aim is to focus the discussion on a deadline	Focus on input and motivation – their unconscious aim is to get input from others or involve them in the discussion
Their goal is the timely accomplishment of a task	Their goal is to get buy-in
Give instructions, provide structure, tell and state direction	Make a statement, describe, explain, suggest and share information
Sound closed when options may be open – may appear decided but may be open to other ideas	Sound open when options may be closed – may appear consultative but want to make the final decision themselves
Comfortable telling people what to do	Comfortable giving information
Give direction and expect the other person to follow it or explain their different perception clearly	Give information and expect the other person to take it into account before acting
Tend not to convey a sense that the other person has a choice – others feel they have to comply	Tend not to convey a sense of urgency – others don't know they are expected to comply
May be seen as bossy	May be seen as indecisive
Stressed when people don't do what they are asked	Stressed by not being included in deciding what to do
May experience the informing style as manipulative	May experience the directing style as autocratic

Adapted from Linda Berens and Susan Nash

Make a note here of which seems to be your preference: _____

The examples below show the directing/informing continuum and the likely style of communication at various points. Clearly, what we say when we want someone to do something is influenced by the demands of the situation and social and cultural norms. However, we naturally have a preference for a directing or informing style and this comes across in the way we express our wishes, particularly when we do not consciously plan how to make a request.

Directing   **Informing**

| I'd like you to write the minutes please | Would you please write the minutes? | We need minutes of this meeting – would you do it please? | It would be good to have minutes of this meeting | We need minutes of the meeting |

In this example, at the directing end it is very clear what the speaker wants and it would be difficult to disagree with it, though a downside could be that the person being instructed resents being told what to do. At the informing end, offering information might result in a willing volunteer coming forward, though a downside could be that it is not clear what the speaker wants.

Here is another example in a domestic situation of the type of statements that may be used at different points on the range.

Directing   **Informing**

| Please change the TV channel | Can you change the channel please? | Can you change the TV channel please as I would like to watch xyz programme? | I was hoping we might watch xyz programme | There's a good programme on the other TV channel |

Again, this example shows a very clear instruction at the directing end. There is no doubt what the speaker wants and the other person is likely to feel they have no option but to comply, though in fact the speaker may be willing to negotiate. At the informing end, the speaker's intention may be to open up a discussion and take the other person's views into account before making a decision, but this is not clear and the other person may be uncertain about what is being asked of them.

In both these examples, the 'blended' style in the middle of the range is likely to be the most effective statement to achieve what the speaker wants, as it combines clarity with explanation.

The preference for directing or informing can be difficult to assess ourselves, because as we grow up, we learn how to get others to do things by express-ing our desires in particular ways. As you assess your style, think about how you would *naturally* express yourself when you are speaking spontaneously, rather than when you are planning what to say and how to say it in advance. Do you naturally give information first, perhaps followed by instruction, or do you naturally give direction first, perhaps followed by explanation?

Here's another example, this time of a couple driving up a motorway and finding there is a traffic jam ahead.

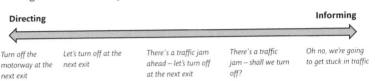

Directing   **Informing**

| Turn off the motorway at the next exit | Let's turn off at the next exit | There's a traffic jam ahead – let's turn off at the next exit | There's a traffic jam – shall we turn off? | Oh no, we're going to get stuck in traffic |

If you were in the passenger seat, what would you say to the driver?

Another way to consider your preference is to think how you would feel if someone used either the directing or informing style with you. In the example above, if you were the driver, would you feel comfortable if you were instructed to turn off? If so, your natural style might be directing. Or would you want some explanation why you should turn off or to be consulted about what to do? If so, your natural style might be informing.

Based on your preference for either directing or informing, consider a situation where you need to influence someone. An example is given to start you off.

Write down an outcome that you want to achieve by influencing somebody else

e.g. You want some friends to agree to a weekend away with you

Write one directing statement and one informing statement to achieve this outcome

Directing: Let's plan to go away for a weekend.

Informing: It would be great if we could spend some time together – how do you fancy going away for a weekend?

Which statement would be most effective in achieving the desired outcome in this situation?

What are the benefits of your preference for someone in your role or situation?
If directing – people are clear on what's expected of them If informing – people get an explanation

What are the pitfalls of your preference for someone in your role or situation?
If directing – people may not respond well to being told what to do If informing – people may be confused about what is required of them

These are some of the benefits and pitfalls of the directing and informing preferences identified by teams at work. As you will see, neither is right or wrong – it depends on what is the most effective behaviour for the circumstances.

	Benefits	Potential pitfalls
Directing preference	Others know what the decisions are Gives impression of being in control Gets things moving Gives clear instruction to others Others may like to be told what to do Helpful in a crisis or when time is short	People may go along with the decision but not take responsibility for it May cut off discussion and input Can appear bossy People may feel they are micro-managed People wait to be told what to do

(Continued)

39

	Benefits	**Potential pitfalls**
Informing preference	Gives information to others	Can appear indecisive
	Allows others to take responsibility	May take too long to make decisions
	Involves others and gets their buy-in	May be seen as weak or wimpy
	Considers all the options	May lack clarity for others
	Helpful when commitment from others is needed	People may not realise what is expected of them
	Helpful when dealing with complex problems	

Aisha was a leader in a manufacturing business who had a directing style. She was on top of everything and continually told her managers what to do and how to do it. Externally, her business was seen as an efficient operation and the business targets were achieved. Internally, her managers felt harried and undervalued. One by one, they moved on to businesses where they could implement some of their own ideas.

Gareth was a leader in a retail business who had an informing style. He was well liked by his team of managers and by the wider staff group. But he felt some of them saw him as a soft touch, as he was usually friendly and showed a high regard for other people and their concerns. Occasionally, he would explode when things hadn't been done the way he wanted, and his team would react with shock, as it appeared out of character. He was coached on how to adopt a more directing style when necessary, so that his team had a clear understanding of his expectations of them.

Communication difficulties often arise when people are different on this dimension. People with the directing style prefer others to communicate clearly what they want. If they are given information without clear direction, they may feel they are being manipulated. People with the informing style prefer others to give them information so they can decide for themselves. If they are given direction without an explanation, they can feel bossed about.

Even when people share the same preference, there is plenty of scope for difficulties in communicating. People who share a preference for directing may experience conflict when they have different views on what should happen because they each naturally sound closed and decisive and it can seem impossible to discuss and reach a consensus. Likewise, people who share a preference for informing may experience conflict when they are discussing options because they each naturally sound open and consultative, and it can be a shock to find the other is not willing to negotiate.

Statements are heard or received differently, depending on the preference of the listener. This also applies to written communication, where sometimes the style can be quite stark. Hence, the advice to think before pressing 'Send'.

Think about when and how your preference for a directing or informing style is most evident.

In what situations, with whom, when?

What is the impact on achieving the outcome you want?

What is the impact on your relationship with the other person?

What opportunities might be missed due to your preference?

If you behaved in line with the opposite preference, what would you do and say in a specific situation?

What result might you get?

Outcome or process focus

When interacting with others to do something, do you focus your attention first on control of the outcome or on the process for moving towards the outcome?

This pair of preferences also underlies the overall patterns of each style. The table describes the two preferences.

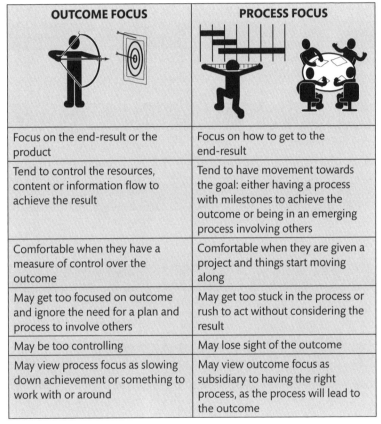

OUTCOME FOCUS	PROCESS FOCUS
Focus on the end-result or the product	Focus on how to get to the end-result
Tend to control the resources, content or information flow to achieve the result	Tend to have movement towards the goal: either having a process with milestones to achieve the outcome or being in an emerging process involving others
Comfortable when they have a measure of control over the outcome	Comfortable when they are given a project and things start moving along
May get too focused on outcome and ignore the need for a plan and process to involve others	May get too stuck in the process or rush to act without considering the result
May be too controlling	May lose sight of the outcome
May view process focus as slowing down achievement or something to work with or around	May view outcome focus as subsidiary to having the right process, as the process will lead to the outcome

Adapted from Linda Berens

In order to get something done, at work or at home, we have to pay attention to both the outcome we want and how to achieve it, or we would fail. But think about where your attention goes first.

Where do you believe your natural tendency lies:

- Towards defining what you want to achieve (an outcome focus)

- Defining the path to achieve it (a process focus), sometimes by engaging others

Make a note here of which seems to be your preference: _____

The four styles and preferences

Each style aligns with a different combination of underlying preferences for either initiating or responding behaviour, and either directing or informing communication. This is shown in the chart below.

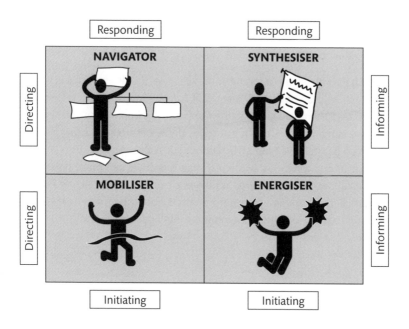

Based on what you have read in this chapter, about the overall patterns and underlying preferences, consider what might be your natural style when you are not being forced by circumstances to adopt a particular style.

My natural style seems to be: _____

In working towards a goal or purpose, two styles naturally focus on having control of the outcome, while the other two focus on the process for movement forward:

- People with the mobiliser style tend to focus on the outcome and push to get closure on the task as soon as possible.

- People with the synthesiser style also focus on the outcome, but with more emphasis on gathering input and information, so they may take longer to get to the outcome.

- People with the navigator style tend to focus on the processes for planning and ensuring all possible risks are covered.

- People with the energiser style tend to focus on the processes for involving and including everyone.

The next chapter gives an overview of each of the four styles – how people come across when they are in each style and what motivations might be driving their behaviour.

If you had difficulty recognising your own style, the descriptions in Chapter 3 will help and you may also want to ask someone who knows you well to read them and give you their opinion. It is important to remember that we can all be flexible in our styles depending on the situation and we often naturally flex our style without conscious thought. Bringing the styles into our conscious awareness means that we can make deliberate choices about how to behave in different circumstances and we can be more skilled at picking up cues from others about their inner drives and respond to them with greater emotional intelligence.

Chapter 3

Being self-aware – the four styles

An emotion involves an urge to move in some fashion

William Moulton Marston[1]

Emotions are part of us and part of almost everything we do. When we interact with others, we experience emotions, though we may not always be aware of them. When we experience an emotion, we usually display some physical sign of it in the body, face, gestures, and the speed and tone of our speech. Excitement may show in faster speech, fear may show in freezing, anger may show in heightened colour, frustration may show in finger tapping, and so on.

These physical signs may or may not be obvious to the people with whom we are communicating. Even if they pick up on the emotional content of our communication, they may not know what feeling underlies it. This link between inner emotion and physical response is a fundamental feature of the four styles. We have an emotional connection to our inner drives and this is expressed physically.

Each of the four styles is associated with specific physical behaviours that are linked to the underlying drives of the style. Most people find that they identify with many characteristics of their self-assessed style as well as some attributes from one or two other styles. This is because they are not hard and fast categories; each style shares some characteristics with other styles, and as I have noted already, we can be flexible in our behaviour depending on the circumstances.

It is also very important to remember that while the styles describe recognisable differences between people, they do not prescribe behaviour. We can choose how we behave in different situations, and our choices are influenced by our upbringing, education and culture, as well as by our inborn personality preferences. Furthermore, we are all unique individuals and there is no model of human behaviour that captures all that variation. But summarising some of these differences between people into recognisable patterns gives us the opportunity to gain more insight into ourselves and options on how to interact with others to achieve better outcomes for everyone.

The names of the four styles reflect the physical energies and the inner drives of each style when interacting with others. The following sections outline what you might see people of each style doing. As you read each one, check that your indication of your own style feels right. More detail is then given in Chapters 4–7. The descriptions are adapted from Linda Berens[2] and Susan Nash.[3]

The Navigator Style

Responding role Directing communication Process focus	People with the navigator style *push for a course of action:*
	• They tend to move in a deliberate way, speak with a measured tone and pace, and appear calm and **focused.** • They create a course of action to achieve the **desired result.** • They make **deliberate** decisions, checking against a thought-through process. • It tends to come naturally to them to plan, monitor, guide and adjust. • They keep the group on track and help to anticipate problems. • They may become stressed when they don't know what is going to happen (or if a plan changes, until they get a new course of action), or if they don't see progress.

At home, many (but not all) people with this style tend to have a planned approach to life. At weekends, they prefer to know what is likely to happen and have a plan for activities. As they have the responding preference, they are unlikely to relish constant interaction with others in their leisure time, and they may want to have plenty of time alone or with small groups of family and friends. Their preference for directing communication means they will sound quite definite about what they want to do, and their family members may not realise that they are more open to discussion than they appear.

At work, they tend to ensure there is a course of action and that everyone is following it. When things go wrong, they want to go back to the plan or process and reset it, making sure everyone knows what the changes are and what their part in it is. They come across to others as deliberate and measured, with a calm and serious demeanour. They can be seen by others as somewhat inflexible in their desire to follow the agreed course of action.

Theresa May, former footballer Alan Shearer and Steve Jobs display some characteristics of the navigator style. In the Simpsons, Lisa has the navigator style – she is organised and self-disciplined and likes to have things under control.

The Mobiliser Style

Initiating role **Directing communication** **Outcome focus** 	People with the mobiliser style *push for action with results:* • They tend to move briskly, speak quite quickly and appear straightforward and **determined.** • They mobilise resources (including people) to get an **achievable result.** • They make **quick** decisions with confidence. • It tends to come naturally to them to decide, direct, mobilise and execute. • They lead the group to the goal and help to get things accomplished. • They may get stressed when others do not share their urgency, or nothing is being accomplished or if they feel out of control.

At home, people with this style tend to have an organised approach to life. They like to feel they have achieved things at weekends and they enjoy activities involving other people – this suits their initiating preference. With the directing preference, they usually have a task and time focus and can be quite decisive about how they want to spend their leisure time. They may communicate this clearly to their family members.

At work, they want to get on with the task as quickly as possible and they often have clear ideas about what needs to be done. They come across as energetic and decisive, composed, confident and in control. They can get frustrated when other people want more discussion before moving ahead and if others resist giving their commitment, they may ultimately withdraw. They may sometimes be seen by others as impatient or demanding.

Alan Sugar, Alex Ferguson and Margaret Thatcher display some of the characteristics of the mobiliser style. Bart Simpson has the mobiliser style – he is direct, speaks his mind and is quick to act.

The Energiser Style	
Initiating role **Informing communication** **Process focus** 	People with the energiser style *push for involvement:* • They tend to move and speak quite quickly and expressively and appear enthusiastic and **engaging.** • They engage others to get an **embraced result.** • They make **collaborative** decisions to ensure buy-in. • It tends to come naturally to them to persuade, energise, facilitate and brainstorm. • They facilitate the group's process and help to raise commitment. • They get stressed when they or others are not involved in what's going on, or if they don't feel accepted.

At home, people with this style tend to be talkative and enthusiastic about their activities. They value social interaction and will usually want to see friends and family at weekends. With the informing preference, they may suggest a lot of options and they will articulate these to the people around them. They take an initiating role and naturally communicate their thoughts to others. They tend to use more words than the other styles, both verbally and in writing.

At work, they like to bring people together, to share and discuss ideas and have fun – they may also be the person who organises social events for colleagues. They come across as outgoing, expressive and friendly. They generally have plenty to say and may feel unappreciated when others do not share their enthusiasm. They can be seen by others as over-enthusiastic or judged as talking too much.

Gary Lineker, Billy Connolly and cyclist Laura Trott display characteristics of the energiser style (Laura's father describes her as bubbly and chatty). Homer Simpson shows some of these attributes – he is outgoing, can be persuasive and charming, likes to be the centre of attention and doesn't like being excluded.

The Synthesiser Style

Responding role Informing communication Outcome focus 	People with the synthesiser style *push for the best result:*
	• They tend to move and speak in an unassuming way, and appear patient and **approachable.**
	• They gather information and input to get the **best result.**
	• They make **consultative** decisions, integrating many sources of input and points of view.
	• It tends to come naturally to them to define, clarify, support and integrate.
	• They support the group's process and help to avoid mistakes.
	• They may get stressed when they don't have enough time or are not given credit for their efforts, or if they are pressed to decide too quickly.

At home, people with this style tend to value harmony and like to be of service to those around them. They are often flexible and willing to accommodate what others want. They like to consider options and naturally consult with others, so when thinking about what to do at the weekend, they are likely to consult and try to get the best possible outcome for everyone. With the informing preference, they may not communicate clearly about what they want to do. As they have the responding preference, they will value some time to themselves at the weekend.

At work, they often want to discuss and explore the issue fully and then decide how to achieve the outcome. Their contribution may be overlooked as they do a lot of activity behind the scenes and don't always articulate what they have done. They come across to others as open and approachable with a quiet and friendly style. They can be seen by others as taking too long and being indecisive and they may have difficulty in getting others to listen to their input.

David Beckham, Andy Murray, J K Rowling and cyclist Jason Kenny (also Laura Trott's husband) display some characteristics of the synthesiser style. (Laura Trott said of Jason Kenny 'he's so laid back, it drives me mad' and his father in law describes him as 'quiet and understated'). Marge Simpson shows the synthesiser style – she is calm, often in the background quietly getting on with things, and she tends to keep the peace and avoid conflict.

Recognising styles

The tables below summarise the typical physical and verbal behaviours (outer appearance) and the specific drives, aims, beliefs, decision-style and stressors (inner motivations) of people of each style for comparison.

Outer Appearance - *when in this style, you might demonstrate this behaviour*

	NAVIGATOR 'What's the plan? Let's get it right'	MOBILISER 'Let's get it done now!'	ENERGISER 'Let's get started and do it together'	SYNTHESISER 'What result do we need?'
VOICE	Calm and measured tone. Measured pace. Pauses to think. Silence feels natural.	Straightforward and direct tone. Fast paced. Pausing feels like a long time. Tends to fill a silence.	Enthusiastic and animated tone. Fast paced. Pausing feels like a long time. Tends to fill a silence.	Gentle and patient tone. Thoughtful pace. Pauses to think. Silence feels natural.
BODY	Light-footed. Puts things down carefully. Moves in a deliberate way to the destination, making adjustments as needed. Pressing and pointing gestures.	Heavy-footed. Puts things down heavily. Moves quickly and directly to the destination. Punching and flicking gestures.	Heavy-footed. Puts things down heavily. Moves in a wavy line to destination, taking in people and information on the way. Slashing and wringing gestures.	Light-footed Puts things down quietly Moves in a wavy line to destination, taking in people and information on the way. Floating and dabbing gestures.
TALKS ABOUT	The plan, who to involve and what to avoid. Reasons and consequences.	Results and actions to be taken. Reasons and consequences.	What's going on with people and who is involved. Points of agreement.	The outcome and information needed. Points of agreement.
MANNER	Formal and business-like	Straightforward and direct	Persuasive and enthusiastic	Unassuming and modest

(Continued)

	NAVIGATOR 'What's the plan? Let's get it right'	MOBILISER 'Let's get it done now!'	ENERGISER 'Let's get started and do it together'	SYNTHESISER 'What result do we need?'
ENERGY	Focused	Determined	Engaging	Approachable
APPEARS	Quiet, calm, intense and serious	Quick-moving, confident and decisive	Expressive, upbeat and casual	Quiet, laid back, friendly and patient

Adapted from Linda Berens, Susan Nash and Andy Cole[4]

Inner Motivations - *when in this style, you might be driven by these factors*

	NAVIGATOR Push for a course of action	MOBILISER Push for action with results	ENERGISER Push for involvement	SYNTHESISER Push for the best result
AIM	To get a **desired** result	To get an **achievable** result	To get an **embraced** result	To get the **best** result possible
DRIVE	Pressing need to **anticipate** obstacles	Urgent need to **accomplish** actions	Urgent need to **involve** others	Pressing need to **integrate** input
CORE BELIEF	It's worth the **effort** to think ahead and reach the goal	It's worth the **risk** to go ahead and act or decide	It's worth the **energy** spent to involve everyone and get them to want to...	It's worth the **time** it takes to integrate and reconcile many inputs
DECISIONS	**Deliberate** and purposeful	**Quick** and expedient	**Collaborative** and engaged	**Consultative** and integrated
PRIORITY	To create a course of action to achieve the desired result	To mobilise resources to get an achievable result	To engage others to get an embraced result	To gather information and input to get the best result
POTENTIAL TALENTS	Planning, monitoring, guiding and adjusting	Deciding, directing, mobilising and executing	Persuading, energising, facilitating and brainstorming	Defining, clarifying, supporting and integrating
WANTS TO	Keep the group on track and help to anticipate problems	Lead the group to a goal and help to get things accomplished	Facilitate the group's process and help to raise commitment	Support the group's process and help to avoid mistakes

	NAVIGATOR Push for a course of action	MOBILISER Push for action with results	ENERGISER Push for involvement	SYNTHESISER Push for the best result
STRESSORS	Not knowing what is likely to happen. Not seeing progress.	Nothing being accomplished. Feeling out of control.	Not being involved in what's going on. Feeling unliked or unaccepted.	Not having enough input, time or credit. Being pressed to decide before they are ready

Adapted from: Linda Berens, Susan Nash

Being aware of your own inner motivations, when you are interacting with others, helps you manage the accompanying behaviours and gives you more chance of achieving your aims. Being aware of what might stress you also helps you manage your behaviours and channel your energy more productively.

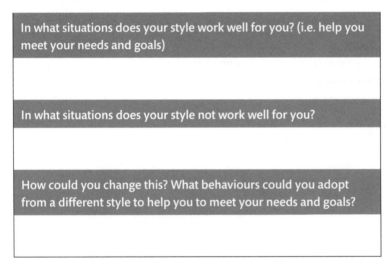

In what situations does your style work well for you? (i.e. help you meet your needs and goals)

In what situations does your style not work well for you?

How could you change this? What behaviours could you adopt from a different style to help you to meet your needs and goals?

Sometimes it is easier to recognise the styles in other people rather than yourself.

Think of people in the public sphere – politicians, characters on TV or celebrities. Who would you put into each style, based on their physical behaviour and how their energy comes across?

(Continued)

**What about people at work or among your family and friends?
Who do you think might fall into each style?**

Each style brings strengths and challenges to interactions with others and each one makes a unique contribution when interacting with others to get things done. In an ideal world, a team at work or family would have someone from each style:

- A Mobiliser to get on quickly with the task

- A Navigator to work out how to reach the goal

- An Energiser to get everyone involved and motivated

- A Synthesiser to consult and get relevant input to achieve the task

A colleague described the contributions of each of the four styles as like a steam train: the Mobiliser sets the destination, the Navigator decides on the route, the Energiser stokes the engine and the Synthesiser oils the wheels.

Now turn to the chapter (4, 5, 6 or 7) that describes what you believe to be your own natural style to explore it in more depth. Or if you would like to think about how to interact with someone from a different style, read the chapters on living and working with each style in Part 2.

Chapter 4

Navigators

It's worth the effort to think ahead to reach the goal

Linda Berens

This chapter covers the navigator style. Note that I use 'Navigator' as a shorthand for 'people with the navigator style'.

| Responding role
Directing communication
Process focus
 | People with the navigator style *push for a course of action:*
• They tend to move in a deliberate way, speak with a measured tone and pace, and appear calm and **focused.**
• They create a course of action to achieve the **desired result.**
• They make **deliberate** decisions, checking against a thought-through process.
• It tends to come naturally to them to plan, monitor, guide and adjust.
• They keep the group on track and help to anticipate problems.
• They may become stressed when they don't know what is going to happen (or if a plan changes, until they get a new course of action), or if they don't see progress. |

Exploring your style

Outer appearance

Generally, when we are communicating with others, unless the occasion has some significance, we do not think about how we come across – how fast or slowly we speak, the expressions on our faces, or how we move our bodies. However, each style has some key characteristics and the table below shows some of the behaviours that might be part of the communication that Navigators transmit to others.

Navigators think 'What's the plan? Let's get it right'	
VOICE	Calm and measured tone
	Measured pace
	Pauses to think
	Silence feels natural

BODY	Light-footed
	Puts things down carefully
	Moves in a deliberate way to the destination, making adjustments as needed
	Pressing and pointing gestures
TALKS ABOUT	The plan, who to involve and what to avoid
	Reasons and consequences
MANNER	Formal and business-like
ENERGY	Focused
APPEARS	Quiet, calm, intense and serious

Adapted from Susan Nash, Linda Berens and Andy Cole

People with the navigator style are usually comfortable giving direction to others – telling or asking other people to do things. They sometimes believe they have the informing preference, as they often start by informing others about the course of action, though in fact this behaviour is an indicator of the directing preference. They often seem definite, though they will negotiate.

This outward behaviour sends messages to the people you are communicating with, so it is worth spending a little time considering what message you might be sending. For example, if you appear intense and distant, the receiver of the message could interpret this in different ways. They might guess that you are thinking hard about something, or they might think you are uninterested and disengaged, or any of a whole range of possible interpretations and inferences. In some circumstances, you might want to create a different impression, for example, by showing through your body language and speed and tone of voice that you are interested and engaged (energiser style), or working urgently to get a result (mobiliser style).

> *Sabina* had the navigator style and was preparing to make a speech at a family event. She had received feedback that she often appeared intense and uncommunicative and this was usually when she was concentrating internally on what she wanted to say, rather than paying attention externally to the audience. Her coach suggested that she make a conscious effort to relax physically and make eye contact with the audience and she even wrote 'SMILE' across the top of her notes to remind herself to connect with the audience. She received much better feedback.

What messages might you send by your demeanour?

Inner motivations

Each style is associated with specific aims, drives, beliefs and decision-making, when working with others to make decisions and achieve results. Those of the navigator style are shown below.

Navigators push for a course of action	
AIM	To get a **desired** result
DRIVE	Pressing need to **anticipate** obstacles
CORE BELIEF	It's worth the **effort** to think ahead and reach the goal
DECISIONS	**Deliberate** and purposeful
PRIORITY	To create a course of action to achieve the desired result
POTENTIAL TALENTS	Planning, monitoring, guiding, adjusting
WANTS TO	Keep the group on track and help to anticipate problems
STRESSORS	Not knowing what is likely to happen
	Not seeing progress

Adapted from Linda Berens, Susan Nash

Being aware of your own inner motivations, when you are interacting with others, helps you manage the accompanying behaviours and gives you more chance of achieving your aims.

> **Shelly** was getting married and going to have a hen party. She knew she wouldn't be able to cope with not knowing what was going to happen, so she told her friends she would organise everything. She felt much happier knowing what to expect.
>
> At work, people with the navigator style tend to be very focused on the topic under discussion. When attending meetings, some may neglect to build relationships with others. **Joshua**, a senior quality engineer, would open his

laptop and ignore the other people in the room until the meeting started. The message he sent by his behaviour was at best that he didn't want to communicate and at worst was seen as lacking interest and enthusiasm. Yet a few simple actions (such as making eye contact and some small talk) completely changed how his colleagues perceived him and he was pleasantly surprised that changing his behaviour meant that people responded more positively to him and to his ideas.

In what situations do you demonstrate these inner drives and beliefs?

Strengths and challenges of the navigator style

Each style brings particular strengths and challenges when interacting with others. These are some that people with the navigator style typically believe they share, taken from workshop discussions.

Strengths:

- Determined focus on the plan to achieve the goal.

- Thinking through the detail of what needs to be done.

- Giving unambiguous direction to others.

- Risk assessment and contingency planning.

- Time management – clear idea of what needs to be done in order to achieve the plan.

- Calm and measured approach.

Challenges:

- To be more flexible to adapt to changes.

- May be slow to respond to others.

- Approach may be time-consuming.

- May lack warmth and may not appear engaged with colleagues.
- May have some difficulty motivating others.

> **What do you see as your strengths and challenges?**

Impact and intention

When we interact with other people, we sometimes have an impact on them which was not what we intended. Often we have a good intention, but how we express it has a negative impact – our positive intentions are lost because of the way we come across to others.

The inner drives show the likely intentions of Navigators when interacting with others. They want to make sure there is a course of action, they want to consider the obstacles and they want everyone to be clear on what is going to happen. These are clearly all positive and well-intentioned aims. However, the actual impact and influence of their behaviour on others can be quite different from what they intended. This can be understood from two perspectives:

- The physical energy and verbal style may not connect well and build rapport with people of other styles.

- The inner drives of people with the other styles are different and therefore they have different priorities in what they consider to be important and worth spending time on.

These two perspectives are covered in the table below.

Building emotional intelligence – self-awareness

A major part of emotional intelligence is being self-aware and knowing how to manage your own behaviour.

IF YOU are in the navigator style.....	
You might come across as...	**So, when working with others...**
Intense and serious	Make an effort to smile and make eye contact
Slow to respond	
Too focused on details and process	Initiate conversation with others, not just about work
Not engaged with the team	Practise speaking up at the right time
Holding back and lacking enthusiasm	Use open body language to appear approachable
Rigid by imposing structure and process	Offer to come back later with your thoughts
Not willing to consider all the options	Speed up your response
	Write things down to help you clarify your thoughts
	Plan how to disclose your thoughts appropriately rather than saying nothing
	Give information rather than direction to show you are open to other ideas
	Make sure you are able to get away and have time to yourself
Your likely inner drives	**So, when working with others...**
To get the desired result	Work with them to clarify the desired result
To make deliberate decisions	
To have a course of action and follow a process	Tell them how you can contribute
	Tell them what you need from them
Likely inner drives of others	**So, when working with them...**
To get an achievable result and make quick decisions (Mobiliser)	Acknowledge their needs
To get an embraced result and make collaborative decisions (Energiser)	Show you recognise the urgency to get things done
	Show you want to involve others and be involved yourself
To get the best result possible and make consultative decisions (Synthesiser)	Allow time for consulting others and be open-minded to options

Anne-Marie, *a senior manager of an IT function in a large organisation, identified with the navigator style and had a strong ability to put systematic plans in place, which was highly valued by her managers. However, she often struggled to get co-operation from others to implement her plans and when in conflict with others, she tended to withdraw. She was extremely task-focused and did not see the value in talking to other people unless it was about a work issue. Learning about the styles helped her to understand that she came across to others as too serious and intense and she recognised the need to spend more time and effort in building relationships. She set aside time in her diary to network with colleagues and found that this paid off when she needed to get their co-operation for her projects.*

Triggers for negative emotions

A key part of emotional intelligence is being aware of our emotions and managing them. But it is difficult to know what is going on in our own minds. Our unconscious drives our behaviour and we use our conscious minds to explain it to ourselves. Our conscious tries to make sense of our actions, thoughts and feelings, but often this is guesswork or rationalisation after the event.

When we feel threatened, the unconscious reacts more quickly than our conscious, sometimes leading us to react in ways that we later wish we hadn't. We respond emotionally before our conscious mind can decide on a more emotionally intelligent reaction. Knowing about our style makes us more aware of our emotions and better able to manage them. For each style there are some specific situations and interactions that might trigger unconscious emotional reactions.

The table below shows the typical triggers for Navigators.

Responding **Directing** **Process focus** 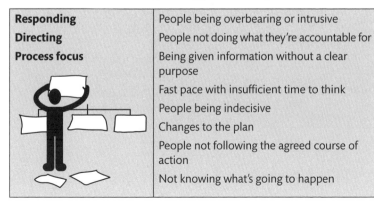	People being overbearing or intrusive
	People not doing what they're accountable for
	Being given information without a clear purpose
	Fast pace with insufficient time to think
	People being indecisive
	Changes to the plan
	People not following the agreed course of action
	Not knowing what's going to happen

Review the triggers for negative emotions and then think about your own behaviour
In what recent situations have you experienced negative emotions?
What did other people do or say that might have triggered your reaction?
How did you respond?
In what other ways could you have responded?
What would be a more effective response if this situation were to recur?

It is not always straightforward to unpick what has triggered an emotional response, as it happens outside our conscious awareness.

Anne-Marie found her negative emotions were triggered when she had to interact with a particular colleague. Most of their interactions involved a crisis situation where he demanded an immediate reaction and resources from her team. She tended to respond by stubbornly sticking to the plan and this escalated into conflict.

(Continued)

From what she told me of his behaviours, we estimated his style as mobiliser, and talked through their interactions from his perspective. His likely strengths would be in dealing with problems quickly, and he would experience stress if nothing appeared to be happening. He could find her navigator style, with minimal communication, lack of immediate reaction to his problems, and desire to stick to the plan, frustrating. Furthermore, with both of them having a directing style, they would both be more inclined to tell each other what to do, rather than explore options.

Thinking about his style in this way gave her insights into her colleague's personality and she worked out strategies to deal more effectively with him, such as responding more quickly and briefing him on her actions. She realised that by changing her own behaviours she could alter the dynamic of their relationship.

Responses to conflict

We have an emotional attachment to our core drives and beliefs, and when we feel that they are not being valued, we experience this as a threat to our self-worth. When this happens, our emotions kick in and we take steps to protect ourselves. The typical initial reaction for people of all styles is firstly to push their own approach harder. We tend to exaggerate the strengths that we normally bring to an interaction and become tunnel-visioned in pursuing our own approach to the exclusion of the others. Mobilisers will push harder to get quick results, Navigators will retreat to sticking to the course of action, Energisers will frantically involve more people and Synthesisers will delay to gather more information.

Unfortunately, this exaggeration of our strengths is counter-productive as it is experienced by others as a threat to their sense of self-worth and they in turn will push harder to fulfil their own drives and they will display an exaggerated form of their own strengths. This inevitably leads to conflict. The situation rapidly becomes polarised, positions become entrenched and conflict escalates. And the possibility of achieving a good outcome recedes.

The initial reaction to conflict for the Navigator is to emphasise the importance of having a course of action. However, when the Navigator's strength in working out a course of action is exaggerated and overdone, it may be seen by others as pedantic, stubborn or rigid.

In this situation, the best tactic for a Navigator is to:

- verbally speed up and use more animated body language (which will build rapport with Mobilisers and Energisers)

- explain how the plan or process will achieve the goal (which will meet the outcome focus of Mobilisers and Synthesisers).

If conflict persists, people react in different ways – they may compete, accommodate, avoid, compromise or collaborate.[1] The Navigator will often adopt the avoid strategy by detaching themselves from the conflict and avoiding further interaction. This can defuse the situation temporarily until it can be dealt with more constructively, or it can lead to the situation stagnating and remaining unresolved.

Remember, you have a choice in how you interact with others. You can adopt a different style and energy pattern if you choose.

> In the case of **Anne-Marie** (see above), she had tended to avoid the conflict with her colleague. She would withdraw from confrontation until she had worked out how to resolve the problem. With a mobiliser style, he probably found this extremely frustrating. She learned to change her conflict avoidance into a more assertive and active response. She acknowledged his urgency and learned to summarise briefly what she was going to do about the problem, even when she hadn't fully thought it all through. She also worked on building a relationship with him so that they had a more positive basis for their interactions.

Think of a recent conflict you have experienced. How did you react? Did you avoid, accommodate, compete, compromise or collaborate?

Was this effective? What might have been a more effective strategy for managing the conflict?

See Chapter 8 for general tips on dealing with conflict.

Stressful situations

Many situations in life are stressful for most of us, irrespective of our style. There are specific stressors that apply to each style, that can occur when we are not able to fulfil our core drives during interactions. Being aware of these stressors means we are more able to manage them.

For Navigators typical stressors are not knowing what's likely to happen and not seeing movement towards the goal. When stressed, they may withdraw or become uncommunicative.

To help, they can try alternative means to gain clarity in direction, focus on what can be influenced or controlled and make an effort to communicate about what they need from others.

> **Daniel's** wife had a serious illness and he needed to leave work earlier than usual to help at home. His core need to follow a course of action drove him to attempt to fulfil all his usual responsibilities at work, as well as taking on tasks and supporting his family at home. He didn't know what was going to happen and he became stressed. Instead of talking to his manager about the problems at home, he withdrew from communicating and no one at work knew he needed help.
>
> This is a typical stress response for Navigators. We used a coaching session with Daniel to plan how and what to communicate about his domestic problems to his manager, colleagues and team members. He acted on the plan and was able to get the support he needed.

What situations cause you stress and how could you alleviate them?

For strategies for dealing with conflict with people of other styles, see Chapters 9–12 in Part 2. For techniques for managing stress and building resilience, read Chapter 17 in Part 3.

Chapter 5

Mobilisers

It's worth the risk to go ahead and act or decide

Linda Berens

This chapter covers the mobiliser style. Note that I use 'Mobiliser' as a shorthand for 'people with the mobiliser style'.

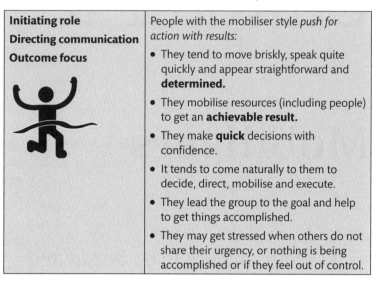

Initiating role Directing communication Outcome focus	People with the mobiliser style *push for action with results:*
	• They tend to move briskly, speak quite quickly and appear straightforward and **determined.**
	• They mobilise resources (including people) to get an **achievable result.**
	• They make **quick** decisions with confidence.
	• It tends to come naturally to them to decide, direct, mobilise and execute.
	• They lead the group to the goal and help to get things accomplished.
	• They may get stressed when others do not share their urgency, or nothing is being accomplished or if they feel out of control.

Exploring your style

Outer appearance

Generally, when we are communicating with others, unless the occasion has some significance, we do not think too much about how we come across – how fast or slowly we speak, the expressions on our face or how we move our body. However, each style has some key characteristics and the table below shows some of the behaviours that are part of the communication that people in the mobiliser style transmit to others.

Mobilisers think 'Let's get it done now!'	
VOICE	Straightforward and direct tone
	Fast-paced
	Pausing feels like a long time
	Tends to fill a silence
BODY	Heavy-footed
	Puts things down heavily
	Moves quickly and directly to the destination
	Punching and flicking gestures

TALKS ABOUT	Results and actions to be taken
	Reasons and consequences
MANNER	Straightforward and direct
ENERGY	Determined
APPEARS	Quick-moving, confident and decisive

Adapted from Linda Berens, Susan Nash, Andy Cole

This outward behaviour sends messages to the people you are communicating with, so it is worth spending a little time considering the message you might be sending. For example, if you appear confident and decisive, the receiver of the message could interpret this in different ways – they might see you as managing a situation competently or as arrogant and over-controlling, or any of a whole range of possible interpretations and inferences. Is this the message you want to send?

If not, what message would you like to transmit through your external behaviour? In some circumstances you might want to create a different impression, for example, by showing through your body language and speed and tone of voice that you are really listening to other people (synthesiser style), or that you want to think through how to overcome obstacles (navigator style).

Carrie was at the airport waiting for her flight. A man walked straight up to her and asked where she was going on holiday. It turned out they were going on the same holiday so he introduced himself and suggested they look out for each other at the baggage reclaim. He walked off without engaging in further conversation. His manner was in the mobiliser style – very straightforward, direct, giving instructions, focused on organising people and resources to get a result. He had achieved what he wanted and didn't see the need for further engagement until they met again at the other end. With Carrie's open and approachable synthesiser style, she would have been happier to have had a little more conversation.

What messages might you send by your demeanour?

Inner motivations

Each style is associated with specific aims, drives, beliefs and decision-making, when working with others to make decisions and achieve results. Those of the mobiliser style are shown below.

Mobilisers push for action with results	
AIM	To get an **achievable** result
DRIVE	Urgent need to **accomplish** actions
CORE BELIEF	It's worth the **risk** to go ahead and act or decide
DECISIONS	**Quick** and expedient
PRIORITY	To mobilise resources to get an achievable result
POTENTIAL TALENTS	Deciding, directing, mobilising, executing
WANTS TO	Lead the group to a goal and help to get things accomplished
STRESSORS	Nothing being accomplished Feeling out of control

Adapted from Linda Berens, Susan Nash

Being aware of your own inner drives, when you are interacting with others, helps you manage the accompanying behaviours and gives you more chance of achieving your aims.

> *Carrie meets **Daisy** on her holiday and they go shopping together. On the way to the shops, there was a choice of routes – Daisy (mobiliser style) said they should walk the most direct way. Carrie (synthesiser style) would have walked the most interesting way if left to her own devices.*
>
> *Carrie wanted suntan lotion. Inside the shop, both women looked at the shelves. Daisy spotted a suitable product, grabbed it off the shelf and thrust it into Carrie's hand, saying 'Here it is, this is what you need.' Carrie would normally have examined the product, weighed up the information on it and compared it with other products, but she felt the pressure from Daisy to get it done quickly, resisted her normal urge and bought it without further ado.*

In what situations do you demonstrate these inner drives and beliefs?

Strengths and challenges

Each style brings particular strengths and challenges to interactions with others. These are some of the strengths and challenges that people with the mobiliser style typically believe they share, taken from workshop discussions.

Strengths:

- Action and energy – they get it done.
- High energy – push rather than pull.
- Target focus, getting results.
- Delivering on time, fast pace.
- Giving structure, clarity and direction.
- Overcoming obstacles.

Challenges:

- Slowing down, reflecting and considering other options.
- Allowing others to speak up and listening to them.
- Making mistakes due to not making time for process and relationships.
- Getting buy in from others so that they take responsibility.
- Managing own frustration when results don't come quickly.

> **What do you see as your strengths and challenges?**
>
>

Impact and intention

The inner drives show the likely intentions of Mobilisers when interacting with others – they want to get things accomplished through people as quickly as possible and achieve the task. These are clearly positive and well-intentioned aims. However, the actual impact and influence of their behaviour on others can be quite different from what they intended. This can be understood from two perspectives:

- The physical energy and verbal style may not connect well and build rapport with people of other styles.

- The inner drives of people with the other styles are different and therefore they have different priorities in what they consider to be important and worth spending time on.

These two perspectives are covered in the table below.

Building emotional intelligence – self-awareness

A major part of emotional intelligence is being self-aware and knowing how to manage your own behaviour.

If YOU are in the mobiliser style.....	
You might come across as...	**So, when working with others...**
Too direct or straightforward	Recognise when you are frustrated
Demanding	Use relaxation techniques such as deep breathing
Impatient	
Unaware of other people's feelings	Step back and give others time to think
	Slow down and let them speak
Unappreciative of other possible outcomes	Consciously listen to them
	Avoid being critical of them and their ideas
Alienating others by controlling resources	Build in time delays to think before you act
	Acknowledge people's feelings
Not listening to team's ideas	Give information rather than direction – don't make all the decisions
Your likely inner drives	**So, when working with others...**
To get an achievable result	Take time to ensure there is buy-in to your ideas
To make quick and expedient decisions	
	Listen to any objections and other ideas
To get things accomplished through people	Defer immediate action – stop the 'urgency' habit
	Step back and reprioritise
	Review your work/life balance

Likely inner drives of others	So, when working with them...
To get the best result possible and make consultative decisions (Synthesiser)	Acknowledge their needs
	Show that you value their contribution and give them time to make it
To get an embraced result and make collaborative decisions (Energiser)	Show you want to involve others and be involved yourself
To get the desired result and make deliberate decisions (Navigator)	Show that you have a plan and a process to reach the goal

Clare's natural style was mobiliser and she wanted to find a way to become more influential with her colleagues without overdoing the mobiliser style – she wanted to engage people rather than instruct them. She realised she needed to make time to talk to people and get to know them better. She decided to try out some of the strategies of other styles, particularly energiser, and she consciously paid attention to involving other people rather than rushing ahead with the task. This awareness of other styles and the option to adopt another style worked well for her in the relationship-building she needed to do to achieve her work goals.

Triggers for negative emotions

A key part of emotional intelligence is being aware of our emotions and managing them. But it is difficult to know what is going on in our own minds. Our unconscious drives our behaviour and we use our conscious minds to explain it to ourselves. Our conscious tries to make sense of our actions, thoughts and feelings, but often this is guesswork or rationalisation after the event.

When we feel threatened, the unconscious reacts more quickly than our conscious, sometimes leading us to react in ways that we later wish we hadn't. We respond emotionally before our conscious mind can decide on a more emotionally intelligent reaction. Knowing our natural style makes us more aware of our emotions and better able to manage them. For each style there are some specific situations and interactions that might trigger unconscious emotional reactions.

The table below shows the typical triggers for Mobilisers.

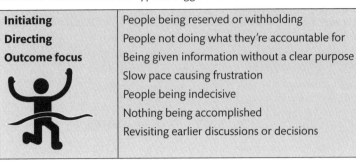

Initiating Directing Outcome focus	People being reserved or withholding
---	People not doing what they're accountable for
	Being given information without a clear purpose
	Slow pace causing frustration
	People being indecisive
	Nothing being accomplished
	Revisiting earlier discussions or decisions

Review the triggers for negative emotions and then think about your own behaviour.

In what recent situations have you experienced these emotions?

What did other people do or say that might have triggered your reaction?

How did you respond?

In what other ways could you have responded?

What would be the most effective response if this situation were to recur?

It is not always straightforward to unpick what has triggered an emotional response, as it happens outside our conscious awareness.

> *Gerry* *was almost a caricature of the mobiliser style – high energy, very active, always doing something or wanting something done by others. He had a tendency to assume that others who didn't exhibit a similar level of energy were lacking in drive or ability. He was concerned about one of his team, Mark, who he felt was reserved and seemed to hold back from the team. We guessed Mark's style was synthesiser. This cast a whole new light on how Gerry perceived him – he saw that Mark's energy was internally focused, that he liked to quietly consult others and gather information in a low-key way before coming up with well researched proposals. Gerry started to recognise his colleague's strengths and we then went on to discuss how he could adapt his own style to connect with Mark's synthesiser style and give him the opportunity to contribute. Gerry decided that he needed 'to rein himself in', to ask questions and listen to the response, to allow pauses in the conversation rather than filling the gaps. These actions enabled Mark to present his thoughts and ideas that previously had not been aired. These were simple actions, with a big impact on the team's effectiveness and individual relationships.*

Responses to conflict

We have an emotional attachment to our core drives and beliefs, and when we feel that they are not being valued, we experience this as a threat to our self-worth. When this happens, our emotions kick in and we take steps to protect ourselves.

The typical initial reaction for people of all styles is firstly to push their own approach harder. We tend to exaggerate the strengths that we normally bring to an interaction and become tunnel-visioned in pursuing our own approach to the exclusion of the others. Mobilisers will push harder to get quick results, Navigators will retreat to sticking to the course of action, Energisers will frantically involve more people and Synthesisers will delay to gather more information.

Unfortunately, this exaggeration of our strengths is counter-productive as it is experienced by others as a threat to their sense of self-worth and they in turn will push harder to fulfil their own drives and they will display an exaggerated form of their own strengths. This inevitably leads to conflict. The situation rapidly becomes polarised, positions become entrenched and conflict escalates. And the possibility of achieving a good outcome recedes.

The initial reaction to conflict for Mobilisers is to emphasise the need to take action to get a result. However, when the Mobiliser's strength in pushing for action is exaggerated and overdone, it may be seen by others as abrasive, rash and aggressive.

In this situation, the best tactic for the Mobiliser is to:

- verbally slow down and ask for input (which will build rapport with Navigators and Synthesisers)

- explain how the plan or process will achieve the goal (which will meet the process focus of Navigators and Energisers and will connect with the informing preference of Synthesisers and Energisers).

If conflict persists, people react in different ways – they may compete, accommodate, avoid, compromise or collaborate.[1] The Mobiliser will often adopt the compete strategy – to assert and fight for what they want. This can be perceived as aggressive, lead to the conflict increasing and resulting in a win–lose outcome.

Remember, you have a choice in how you interact with others. You can adopt a different style and energy pattern if you choose.

At work, people with the mobiliser style have the potential to contribute by pushing ahead to achieve the task. However, their approach may be seen as railroading by others and they may not listen to and get the buy-in from their colleagues.

I once inadvertently put four Mobilisers together in a workshop to carry out a task – they spent the whole time arguing about the approach and shouting over each other. Despite this, they did achieve the task, perhaps because each person's desire to get a result (any result) outweighed how wedded each of them were to their own solutions.

Had there been anyone in the group with other styles, they would have found it difficult to work in the competitive atmosphere created by the mobiliser styles.

> Think of a recent conflict you have experienced. How did you react? Did you avoid, accommodate, compete, compromise or collaborate?

> Was this effective? What might have been a more effective strategy for managing the conflict?

See Chapter 8 for general tips on dealing with conflict.

Stressful situations

Many situations in life are stressful for most of us, irrespective of our style. However, there are specific stressors that apply particularly to each style, which occur when we are not able to fulfil our core drives during interactions. Being aware of these stressors means we are more able to manage them.

For Mobilisers typical stressors are nothing being accomplished and feeling out of control. When stressed, they may become demanding or angry, blame others and disengage or even walk out.

To help, they can defer immediate action – stop the 'urgency' habit, step back and reprioritise, and take time out.

> *Mohammed felt he spent a lot of time in meetings where the same topics would come up and be revisited, with no clear decisions being finalised. He described himself as very frustrated and talked about how stressed he felt in these meetings. He identified with the mobiliser style and knew his comfort zone was to have decisions made quickly and things being accomplished. The constant revisiting of topics was taking him out of his comfort zone and he was experiencing negative emotions that he acknowledged were coming*

(Continued)

out as impatience and sarcasm, and sometimes withdrawal, which in turn had a negative impact on his colleagues.

We discussed the possible styles of his colleagues, what might be driving their behaviour and the benefits these could bring to the team and the organisation. He was able to shift to take their perspective and finally, he recognised that 'the problem is me, not them' and that he could find ways to manage his frustrations and allow them to make their contributions.

What situations cause you stress and how could you alleviate them?

For strategies for dealing with conflict with people of other styles, see Chapters 9–12 in Part 2. For techniques for managing stress and building resilience, see Chapter 17 in Part 3.

Chapter 6

Energisers

It's worth the energy to involve everyone and get them to want to....

Linda Berens

This chapter covers the energiser style. Note that I use 'Energiser' as a shorthand for 'people with the energiser style'.

Initiating role Informing communication Process focus 	People with the energiser style *push for involvement:* • They tend to move and speak quite quickly and expressively and appear enthusiastic and **engaging.** • They engage others to get an **embraced result.** • They make **collaborative** decisions to ensure buy-in. • It tends to come naturally to them to persuade, energise, facilitate and brainstorm. • They facilitate the group's process and help to raise commitment. • They get stressed when they or others are not involved in what's going on, or if they don't feel accepted.

Exploring your style

Outer appearance

Generally, when we are communicating with others, unless the occasion has some significance, we do not think about how we come across – how fast or slowly we speak, the expressions on our faces, or how we move our bodies. However, each style has some key characteristics and the table below shows some of the behaviours that are part of the communication that people in the energiser style transmit to others.

Energisers think 'Let's get started and let's do it together'	
VOICE	Enthusiastic and animated tone
	Fast-paced
	Pausing feels like a long time
	Tends to fill a silence
BODY	Heavy-footed
	Puts things down heavily
	Moves in a wavy line to destination, taking in people and information on the way
	Slashing and wringing gestures

TALKS ABOUT	What's going on with people and who is involved
	Points of agreement
MANNER	Persuasive and enthusiastic
ENERGY	Engaging
APPEARS	Expressive, upbeat, casual

Adapted from Linda Berens, Susan Nash, Andy Cole

This outward behaviour sends messages to the people you are communicating with, so it is worth spending a little time considering what message you might be sending. For example, if you appear 'expressive of your thoughts or emotions', the receiver of the message could interpret this in different ways – they might welcome the openness or may find it overpowering, or any of a whole range of possible interpretations and inferences. In some circumstances, you might want to create a different impression, for example, by showing through your body language and speed and tone of voice that you are focused on getting a quick result (mobiliser style) or that you are listening carefully and considering other points of view (synthesiser style).

> **Marion** was on holiday with a group of people she hadn't met previously. Each time she met someone new, she quickly fell into conversation with them, found lots to talk to them about and came across as very chatty and communicative. During the holiday, she was often in the midst of many social activities, and when she talked about her life at home, she commented that 'I like to bring people together who don't know each other'. She knew from previous feedback that sometimes she could be too talkative and so she made a conscious effort to pause to let others in on the conversation.

What messages do you send in your demeanour?

Inner motivations

Each style is associated with specific aims, drives, beliefs and decision-making, when working with others to make decisions and achieve results. Those of the energiser style are shown below.

Energisers push for involvement	
AIM	To get an **embraced** result
DRIVE	Urgent need to **involve** others
CORE BELIEF	It's worth the **energy** spent to involve everyone and get them to want to...
DECISIONS	**Collaborative** and engaged
PRIORITY	To engage others to get an embraced result
POTENTIAL TALENTS	Persuading, energising, facilitating, brainstorming
WANTS TO	Facilitate the group's process and help to raise commitment
STRESSORS	Not being involved in what's going on
	Feeling unliked or unaccepted

Adapted from Linda Berens, Susan Nash

Being aware of your own inner drives, when you are interacting with others, helps you manage the accompanying behaviours and gives you more chance of achieving your aims.

> **Tom** *was the manager of a car dealership and his top priority was to engage the people who worked for him. He thrived on communicating and his energy and motivation when he did it was visible to others. He ran regular whole-site face-to-face briefings, got staff involved in charity events, had regular team meetings, networked with his colleagues running other dealerships, sent personal notes to keep in touch with people, and he used social media channels to communicate with staff and customers. He spent a higher proportion of his time involving others than his colleagues in similar businesses. Most of the time he felt that the effort was worthwhile, though occasionally he felt disappointed when people didn't respond with enthusiasm.*

In what situations do you demonstrate these inner drives and beliefs?

Strengths and challenges of the energiser style

Each style brings particular strengths and challenges when interacting with others. These are some that people with the energiser style typically believe they share, taken from workshop discussions:

Strengths:

- Energy and enthusiasm.

- Positive – seeing options and optimistic about the outcome.

- Finding the possible, no matter what.

- Engaging with everyone and helping others to join in.

- Sharing ideas and thoughts.

- Motivating the team to commit to action.

Challenges:

- Allowing others to fully convey their views (without doing it with them).

- Making a concise conclusion and knowing when to stop.

- Having a clear plan and sense of direction.

- Staying focused on achieving the goal.

- Not getting discouraged if others are not enthusiastic.

> **What do you see as your strengths and challenges?**
>
>
>

Impact and intention

When we interact with other people, we sometimes have an impact on them which was not what we had intended. Often we have a good intention, but how we express it has a negative impact – our positive intentions are lost because of the way we come across to others.

The inner drives show the likely intentions of Energisers when interacting with others. They want to involve others and get everyone to contribute towards achieving the goal. These are clearly all positive and well-intentioned aims. However, the actual impact and influence of their behaviour on others can be quite different from what they intended. This can be understood from two perspectives:

- The physical energy and verbal style may not connect well and build rapport with people of other styles.

- The inner drives of people with the other styles are different and therefore they have different priorities in what they consider to be important and worth spending time on.

These two perspectives are covered in the table below.

Building emotional intelligence – self-awareness

A major part of emotional intelligence is being self-aware and knowing how to manage your own behaviour.

If YOU are in the energiser style.....	
You might come across as...	**So, when working with others...**
Overly optimistic	Moderate your enthusiasm to be credible
Lacking focus on the task	Find someone to act as a sounding board so you can talk things out
Too talkative	
Easily discouraged	Slow down and think things through
Not mindful of the details or the need for structure and planning	Ask for input from others and listen to it
	Focus on the key individuals who are engaged and involved
Frenetic by wanting to involve and enthuse others	Be realistic that not everyone can be engaged
Throwing in too many ideas	Understand that people may be thinking options through and this does not mean they are uninterested or uncommitted
	Give direction rather than information – be explicit about what you want
	Ask someone for support and guidance
	Consciously limit how much you say

Your likely inner drives	So, when working with others...
To get an embraced result	Remind yourself that you don't have to be involved
To make collaborative decisions	Focus your energy where you can help to move things forward
To persuade and involve others	Reframe negative reactions – put them in perspective
	Recognise when consensus is not needed
	Use techniques to restore your self-belief, such as positive mental thinking

Likely inner drives of others	So, when working with them...
To get the best result possible and make consultative decisions (Synthesiser)	Acknowledge their needs
	Show you value their contribution and give them time to make it
To get an achievable result and make quick decisions (Mobiliser)	Show you recognise the urgency to get things done
To get the desired result and make deliberate decisions (Navigator)	Show you have a course of action and a process to reach the goal

Casie was a manager in a call centre who had the energiser style. She created a lively and fun atmosphere in her team and had a high regard for her team members and concern for their well-being. She was liked by the team and enjoyed organising social events and things to make the working day go well. She spent so much energy on engaging others that she didn't leave time for seeing things through to completion and her team were sometimes unsure of their priorities as tasks were not followed up. This was a blind-spot for her and she had to work on this in order to be fully effective in her role.

Triggers for negative emotions

A key part of emotional intelligence is being aware of our emotions and managing them. But it is difficult to know what is going on in our own minds. Our unconscious drives our behaviour and we use our conscious minds to explain it to ourselves. Our conscious tries to make sense of our actions, thoughts and feelings, but often this is guesswork or rationalisation after the event.

When we feel threatened, the unconscious reacts more quickly than our conscious, sometimes leading us to react in ways that we later wish we hadn't. We respond emotionally before our conscious mind can decide on a more emotionally intelligent reaction. Knowing about our style makes us more aware of our emotions and better able to manage them. For each style there are some specific situations and interactions that might trigger unconscious emotional reactions.

The table below shows the typical triggers for Energisers.

Initiating **Informing** **Process focus** 	People being reserved or withholding
	People not listening to their input
	Being told what to do without an explanation
	Slow pace causing frustration
	People being bossy
	Others not showing enthusiasm
	Not feeling involved or being left out

Review the triggers for negative emotions and then think about your own behaviour

In what recent situations have you experienced these emotions?

What did other people do or say that might have triggered your reaction?

How did you respond?

In what other ways could you have responded?
What would be a more effective response if this situation were to recur?

It is not always straightforward to unpick what has triggered an emotional response, as it happens outside our conscious awareness.

> **Sasha** (Energiser) and her husband Matt (Navigator) were planning a home improvement project. Sasha was excited about it and looking forward to working on the plans together, but Matt wanted to work the plan out by himself. She felt left out and unappreciated while he wanted to put together a thorough plan without any distractions. Knowing about their different styles enabled them to discuss how they each felt and they came up with a solution that worked for them both.

Responses to conflict

We have an emotional attachment to our core drives and beliefs, and when we feel that they are not being valued, we experience this as a threat to our self-worth. When this happens, our emotions kick in and we take steps to protect ourselves.

The typical initial reaction for people of all styles is firstly to push their own approach harder. We tend to exaggerate the strengths that we normally bring to an interaction and become tunnel-visioned in pursuing our own approach to the exclusion of the others. Mobilisers will push harder to get quick results, Navigators will retreat to sticking to the course of action, Energisers will frantically involve more people and Synthesisers will delay to gather more information.

Unfortunately, this exaggeration of our strengths is counter-productive as it is experienced by others as a threat to their sense of self-worth and they in turn will push harder to fulfil their own drives and they will display an exaggerated form of their own strengths. This inevitably leads to conflict. The situation rapidly becomes polarised, positions become entrenched and conflict escalates. And the possibility of achieving a good outcome recedes.

The initial reaction to conflict for Energisers is to conciliate. However, when the Energiser's strength in involving and energising others is exaggerated and overdone, it may be seen by others as frenetic, intrusive or indiscriminate.

In this situation, the best tactic for an Energiser is to:

- verbally slow down (which will build rapport with Navigators and Synthesisers)

- state the goal and clarify who needs to be involved to achieve the goal (which will meet the outcome focus of Mobilisers and Synthesisers) and clarify the process for moving ahead (which will meet the needs of Navigators).

If conflict persists, people react in different ways – they may compete, accommodate, avoid, compromise or collaborate.[1] The Energiser will often adopt the 'compromise' strategy – perhaps give up some of what they want in order to reach agreement and maintain harmony. This can help to move forward, but may also delay the resolution process.

Remember, you have a choice in how you interact with others. You can adopt a different style and energy pattern if you choose.

Lily, a senior manager in a utility business, often came up with new ideas at work and explained them enthusiastically to her colleagues. When they challenged her thinking or were critical, she tended to push back, speaking more quickly and loudly and giving them even more information. If that wasn't successful, she would eventually back down and leave disappointed and resentful. She was coached to take a different approach, in which she first listened to their concerns and then responded to them calmly and slowly. She found that this created a collaborative climate and led to her ideas (sometimes with modification) being taken on.

> Think of a recent conflict you have experienced. How did you react? Did you avoid, accommodate, compete, compromise or collaborate?

> Was this effective? What might have been a more effective strategy for managing the conflict?

See Chapter 8 for general tips on dealing with conflict.

Stressful situations

Many situations in life are stressful for most of us, irrespective of our style. However, there are specific stressors that apply particularly to each style that can occur when we are not able to fulfil our core drives during interactions. Being aware of these stressors means we are more able to manage them.

For Energisers, typical stressors are feeling not liked, unappreciated, not involved, and people not appearing to be engaged or interested. When stressed, they may feel panicky, or become louder and more expressive, or even withdraw completely.

To help, they can remind themselves they don't have to be involved, and focus their energy where they can help to move things forward.

> *Jasmine* loved working with others and feeling a sense of everyone moving forward together. Sometimes her desire to be involved in everything meant she put herself under too much pressure or ended up letting other people down. In order to keep her work to manageable levels, she had to learn how to say no and to be content with not always being involved.

> **What situations cause you stress and how could you alleviate them?**

For strategies for dealing with conflict with people of other styles, see Chapters 9–12 in Part 2. For techniques for managing stress and building resilience, see Chapter 17 in Part 3.

Chapter 7

Synthesisers

It's worth the time to integrate and reconcile many inputs

Linda Berens

This chapter covers the synthesiser style. Note that I use 'Synthesiser' as a shorthand for 'people with the synthesiser style'.

Responding role Informing communication Outcome focus 	People with the synthesiser style *push for the best result:* <ul><li>They tend to move and speak in an unassuming way, and appear patient and **approachable.**</li><li>They gather information and input to get the **best result.**</li><li>They make **consultative** decisions, integrating many sources of input and points of view.</li><li>It tends to come naturally to them to define, clarify, support and integrate.</li><li>They support the group's process and help to avoid mistakes.</li><li>They may get stressed when they don't have enough time or are not given credit for their efforts, or if they are pressed to decide too quickly.</li></ul>

Exploring your style

Outer appearance

Generally, when we are communicating with others, unless the occasion has some significance, we do not think about how we come across – how fast or slowly we speak, the expressions on our faces, or how we move our bodies. However, each style has some key characteristics and the table below shows some of the behaviours that are part of the communication that people in the synthesiser style transmit to others.

Synthesisers think 'What result do we need?	
VOICE	Gentle and patient tone
	Thoughtful pace
	Pauses to think
	Silence feels natural
BODY	Light-footed
	Puts things down quietly
	Moves in a wavy line to destination, taking in people and information on the way
	Floating and dabbing gestures

TALKS ABOUT	The outcome and information needed
	Points of agreement
MANNER	Unassuming and modest
ENERGY	Approachable, open
APPEARS	Quiet, laid back, friendly and patient

Sources: Linda Berens, Susan Nash, Andy Cole

This outward behaviour sends messages to the people you are communicating with, so it is worth spending a little time considering what message you might be sending. For example, if you appear quiet and laid back, the receiver of the message could interpret this in different ways. They might see you as considerate and approachable or may assume that you have nothing to contribute, or any of a whole range of possible interpretations and inferences.

Is this the message you want to send? If not, what message would you like to transmit through your external behaviour? In some circumstances you might want to create a different impression, for example, by showing through your body language and speed and tone of voice that you are working urgently to get a result (mobiliser style), or that you want to engage and enthuse people (energiser style).

> *Jenny's* demeanour came across as unassertive and she found it difficult to make her points heard when in discussion with others. She learned how to signal through her body language that she had something to say, such as by shifting her body, leaning forward, taking in a breath, moving her hand – a bit like attracting the attention of a waiter in a restaurant.
>
> She also worked on how to express herself more concisely and assertively, by planning and summarising what she wanted to say in advance, speaking more loudly and lowering her tone. She also used assertive phrases such as 'I think..., I want..., my opinion is...' These small changes helped her to have a bigger impact.

What messages do you send by your demeanour?

Inner motivations

Each style is associated with specific aims, drives, beliefs, and decision-making when working with others to make decisions and achieve results. Those of the synthesiser style are shown below.

Synthesisers push for the best result	
AIM	To get the **best** result possible
DRIVE	Pressing need to **integrate** input
CORE BELIEF	It's worth the **time** it takes to integrate and reconcile many inputs
DECISIONS	**Consultative** and integrated
PRIORITY	To gather information and input to get the best result
POTENTIAL TALENTS	Defining, clarifying, supporting and integrating
WANTS TO	Support the group's process and help to avoid mistakes
STRESSORS	Not having enough input, time or credit Being pressed to decide too quickly

Adapted from Linda Berens, Susan Nash

Being aware of your own inner drives, when you are interacting with others, helps you manage the accompanying behaviours and gives you more chance of achieving your aims. Similarly, being consciously aware of your stressors when your needs are not met means that you can manage your reactions more constructively.

> **Jim,** a newly appointed leader with the synthesiser style, was people-oriented, liked by his team and successful at getting results. He had been promoted internally and was aware that he needed to develop other skills and behaviours in order to be successful at the more senior level. Learning about the styles helped him to crystallise his key strengths, challenges and priorities for action. He knew that his approachable manner could be seen as lacking authority and that his consultative style could be seen as indecisive, so he consciously adapted his behaviour to ensure that he was firm and fair with others and kept them informed about key decisions.

In what situations do you demonstrate these inner drives and beliefs?

Strengths and challenges of the synthesiser style

Each style brings particular strengths and challenges to interactions with others. These are some of the strengths and challenges that people with the synthesiser style typically believe they share, taken from workshop discussions:

Strengths:

- Focused on the outcome – to deliver the best result.

- Consultative style, involving others.

- Patience, listening to others, noticing people and the atmosphere in the room.

- Integrating ideas and information.

- Completing the jigsaw, linking to the bigger picture, considering all the options.

- Calm and approachable.

Challenges:

- Being heard and getting views across to others.

- Feeling rushed to closure.

- Perfectionism – trying to get the best result rather than a good enough result.

- May appear indecisive or weak.

- Approach may be time-consuming.

What do you see as your strengths and challenges?

Impact and intention

When we interact with other people, we sometimes have an impact on them which was not what we intended. Often we have a good intention, but how we express it has a negative impact – our positive intentions are lost because of the way we have come across to others.

The inner drives show the likely intentions of Synthesisers when interacting with others – they want to make sure all the relevant information has been considered and that a full range of options has been explored, in order to get the best result, not just a 'good enough' result. These are clearly all positive and well-intentioned aims. However, the actual impact and influence of their behaviour on others can be quite different from what they intended. This can be understood from two perspectives:

- The physical energy and verbal style may not connect well and build rapport with people of other styles.

- The inner drives of people with the other styles are different and therefore they have different priorities in what they consider to be important and worth spending time on.

These two perspectives are covered in the table below.

Building emotional intelligence – self-awareness

A major part of emotional intelligence is being self-aware and knowing how to manage your own behaviour.

If YOU are in the synthesiser style.....

You might come across as...	So, when working with others...
Unassertive	Ask for time and space to work out your thoughts
Going into too much depth	
Taking too much time and meandering around the topic	Find out and think about meeting topics ahead of time
Lacking clarity of direction	Use more expressive body language when you have a point to make
Being slow to decide and to act	
Sub-servient by accommodating too many needs	Be more assertive – speak more confidently
	Summarise and make specific, pertinent points
Making things too complicated	Find ways to get heard in a group and to be listened to without being interrupted
	Break the task into smaller chunks
	Clarify where decisions are needed now and which areas can wait for more data
	Give direction rather than information – be explicit about what you want

Your likely inner drives	So, when working with others...
To get the best result possible	Be prepared to compromise on the goal
To make consultative decisions	Agree with them how the consultation process will work and who will make the decision
To gather input to get the best quality outcome	
	Tell others how their input was included in the final decision
	Reward yourself when you achieve something that's important to you

Likely inner drives of others	So, when working with them...
To get an achievable result and make quick decisions (Mobiliser)	Acknowledge their needs
	Show you recognise the urgency to get things done
To get an embraced result and make collaborative decisions (Energiser)	Show you want to involve others and be involved yourself
To get the desired result and make deliberate decisions (Navigator)	Show that you have a course of action and a process to reach the goal

Synthesisers believe that it is worth spending time to integrate all the information to get the best result possible – this strongly held belief can slow the process down, frustrate others and lead to action being taken too late or not at all – hardly a good outcome. Some years ago, I was part of a team working on a leadership programme in a large IT company. I have the synthesiser style and one of my colleagues was a Mobiliser. At one meeting we had a major clash. I wanted us to design a world-class leadership programme, (get the best result possible) while she wanted to ensure we met the deadline (get an achievable result). She felt it would take too much time to get the highest quality outcome and we would miss the deadline, while I felt her desire to rush ahead would be a missed opportunity to offer something of real value. In the end the need to get something done by the deadline won – an understandable result in a business organisation. I'm convinced that if we had understood our respective styles and drives, we would have found ways to manage our conflict more constructively and probably got a better outcome for the organisation too.

Triggers for negative emotions

A key part of emotional intelligence is being aware of and able to manage our emotions. But it is difficult to know what is going on in our own minds. Our unconscious drives our behaviour and we use our conscious minds to explain it to ourselves. Our conscious tries to make sense of our actions, thoughts and feelings, but often this is guesswork or rationalisation after the event.

When we feel threatened, the unconscious reacts more quickly than our conscious, sometimes leading us to react in ways that we later wish we hadn't. We respond emotionally before our conscious mind can decide on a more emotionally intelligent reaction. Knowing about the styles makes us more aware of our emotions and better able to manage them. For each style there are some specific situations and interactions that might trigger unconscious emotional reactions.

The table below shows the typical triggers for Synthesisers for negative emotions when interacting with others.

Responding Informing Outcome focus 	People being overbearing or intrusive
	People not listening to their input
	Being told what to do without an explanation
	Fast pace with insufficient time to think
	People being bossy
	Not having enough time to integrate all the information
	Not being given credit for their contribution
	Being forced to make a decision before they are ready

Review the triggers for negative emotions and then think about your own behaviour

In what recent situations have you experienced these emotions?

What did other people do or say that might have triggered your reaction?

How did you respond?

In what other ways could you have responded?

(Continued)

> **What would be a more effective response if this situation were to recur?**
>
>
>
>

It is not always straightforward to unpick what has triggered an emotional response, as it happens outside our conscious awareness.

> *Jane* *wrote into a newspaper's employment advice column with a classic Synthesiser's problem: her contributions at meetings were ignored, someone else would make the same suggestion and be listened to, her completed work was not acknowledged and she found it difficult to get into the discussions while others talked over or interrupted each other. This was having a negative impact on her confidence and self-esteem. She was not having the opportunity to give her input or get credit for it – essential motivators for Synthesisers. The advice given by the columnist and readers included to lower the pitch of her voice, raise the volume, write down first what she wanted to say, and to speak calmly and continuously. They also suggested 'flagging' that she was going to say something important by starting assertively with a phrase such as 'I have a very good idea…would you like to hear it?'*
>
> *This case illustrates that you can't change other people's behaviour – you can only change your own, but by changing your own you will get a different response.*

Responses to conflict

We have an emotional attachment to our core drives and beliefs, and when we feel that our core drives are not being valued, we experience this as a threat to our self-worth. When this happens our emotions kick in and we take steps to protect ourselves.

The typical initial reaction for people of all styles is firstly to push their own approach harder. We tend to exaggerate the strengths that we normally bring to an interaction and become tunnel-visioned in pursuing our own approach to the exclusion of the others. Mobilisers will push harder to get quick results, Navigators will retreat to sticking to the course of action, Energisers will frantically involve more people and Synthesisers will delay to gather more information.

Unfortunately, this exaggeration of our strengths is counter-productive as it is experienced by others as a threat to their sense of self-worth and they in turn will push harder to fulfil their own drives and they will display an exaggerated form of their own strengths. This inevitably leads to conflict. The situation rapidly becomes polarised, positions become entrenched and conflict escalates. And the possibility of achieving a good outcome recedes.

The initial reaction to conflict for Synthesisers is to emphasise the importance of getting enough input and information. However, when the Synthesiser's strength in gathering and integrating information is exaggerated and overdone, they may be seen by others as indecisive, compliant and unpredictable.

In this situation, the best tactic for the Synthesiser is to:

- verbally speed up (which will build rapport with Mobilisers and Energisers)

- explain how the process being followed will achieve the goal (which will meet the outcome focus of Mobilisers and the process focus of Navigators)

- explain how people's involvement is being managed and their views being considered (to meet the involvement needs of Energisers)

If conflict persists, people react in different ways – they may compete, accommodate, avoid, compromise or collaborate.[1] The Synthesiser will often adopt the accommodate strategy – they will comply and submit to what the other person wants. This can lead to a lose-win outcome if they neglect their own concerns completely.

Remember, you have a choice in how you interact with others. You can adopt a different style and energy pattern if you choose.

Matthew was on a skiing holiday at the end of which his standard of skiing was graded. He was upset with the grading as he felt it was lower than warranted by his performance. He was also annoyed that another person in the group who skied at the same standard had been graded higher. This person was someone who tended to push himself to the front and be visible in the group, while Matthew tended to fit in with the others and did not draw attention to himself. At first he fumed in silence, but after speaking

(Continued)

> quietly to one or two friends, who confirmed his view of his ski standard, he
> decided to raise it with the leader who had given the grading and he
> achieved the upgrading he wanted.
>
> Matthew had been stressed by not being given credit for his ability, had
> overcome his synthesiser instinct to accommodate and found the courage to
> be assertive in standing up for his own needs – with a positive outcome.

Think of a recent conflict you have experienced.

How did you react? Did you avoid, accommodate, compete, compromise or collaborate?

Was this effective? What might have been a more effective strategy for managing the conflict?

See Chapter 8 for general tips on dealing with conflict.

Stressful situations

Many situations in life are stressful for most of us, irrespective of our style. However, there are specific stressors that apply to each style, that can occur when we are not able to fulfil our core drives during interactions. Being aware of these stressors means we are more able to manage them.

For Synthesisers, typical stressors are not having enough input, time or credit and being pushed to decide before they are ready. When stressed, they may become quiet and appear to agree with the other person, avoid overt conflict and take a stubborn position if it is something really important to them.

To help, they can break the task into smaller chunks so that progress can be demonstrated, clarify where decisions are needed and which areas can wait, speak up about what they have done, and recognise that sometimes a timely good enough result is better than a late best result.

> *Ella wanted a new kitchen but was overwhelmed with too much choice of styles, suppliers and installers. She needed time to explore all the options and compare each one to make sure she made the best decision – she didn't feel ready to decide until she had done this, but at the same time she was aware that she didn't have much spare time to investigate options, and she wanted the new kitchen soon. She felt stressed and anxious and almost ready to give up on the whole idea. Her friend suggested she break the task down into manageable chunks, prioritised by time and tackle it bit by bit. They came up with a workable plan, and three months later, Ella had her new kitchen.*

What situations cause you stress and how could you alleviate them?

For strategies of dealing with conflict with people of other interaction styles, see Chapters 9–12 in Part 2. For techniques of managing stress and building resilience, see Chapter 17 in Part 3.

Part 2

How to recognise styles in other people

Chapter **8**

Being aware of others

The real practical output is how we engage with other people and build relationships

Martin Newman[1]

Having self-awareness and the ability to manage your own emotions is one half of the emotional quotient (EQ) equilibrium. The other half is awareness of others and being able to build relationships with them. This section of the book focuses on this side of the EQ equilibrium.

We infer what other people are thinking and feeling from what we perceive of their external behaviour, what they do and say, their tone of voice and their facial expressions. We saw in Chapter 1 that perception of other people is prone to distortion and error and that it is almost impossible to know what is going on in the minds of other people. Even when we know people well, we often get it wrong.

We make assumptions about other people and one of the most common assumptions and fundamental errors is to assume that everyone is 'like me'. We assume that how *we* might think or feel in a particular situation is what *they* are thinking or feeling too. We assume that other people share our values, beliefs and motivations. We assume that what drives our behaviour, when we communicate with others, is the same as what drives their behaviour and we are often surprised when they don't see things the way we do. 'Like me' is a common problem in selection interviewing. We find it easier to build rapport with people who are similar to ourselves, with a similar background and interests – but this does not mean they are the best person for the job.

Our inferences about other people guide how we react and respond to them. Our behaviour sends messages to them and they react accordingly. This can be a virtuous circle of increasing rapport and empathy or a downward spiral of fewer and fewer productive behaviours. This process occurs quickly, often outside our conscious control. However, if we pause to think, we can choose our response.

How the styles can help

Knowing about the styles is a shortcut to appreciating what might be going on for someone and responding to it more appropriately. We have already seen that there is a correlation between the physical energy displayed and the inner drives of that behaviour. So, if we see someone rushing around, speaking and moving quickly, using chopping hand gestures, this might indicate that they have the mobiliser energy and are being driven by an urgent need to accomplish something. An appropriate response in this situation might be to also start moving and speaking quickly, to show that you appreciate the urgency of the situation.

Similarly, if we see someone looking intense and serious, moving deliberately, using pressing and pointing gestures, speaking at a measured pace, this might indicate that they have the navigator energy and are being driven by a pressing need to anticipate. An appropriate response in this situation might be to slow down your own speech, listen to what they have to say and acknowledge the need for an agreed course of action.

If we see someone speaking enthusiastically with expressive gestures, engaging people and pulling them in, then it is likely they have the energiser energy and are being driven by an urgent need to involve others. Here, an appropriate response would be to respond with enthusiasm, nodding agreement, and building on their ideas.

Finally, if we see someone looking calm with an open body posture, touching things lightly and speaking quietly, then it is likely that they have the synthesiser energy and are being driven by a pressing need to integrate information. An appropriate response would be to give them time, to listen to them, to answer their questions and to keep options open.

Becoming more aware of others

We pick up cues all the time about other people, often without being consciously aware. Making this process more conscious means that we are more likely to interpret the cues correctly and respond skilfully, rather than responding automatically without conscious thought.

We can improve our skills in picking up on others' behaviour through practice.

In Chapter 3 (Table 2 in the Appendix) there is a table describing the outer appearance of each style. Review this and use it in conjunction with the observation sheet below to hone your skills in picking up on other people's styles. You could start by watching people being interviewed on TV.

Physical or verbal characteristics	Examples/comments
VOICE Tone Pace Pausing Silence	
BODY Light or more grounded Speed Direct or indirect movement Gestures	
TALKS ABOUT	
MANNER	
ENERGY	
APPEARS	
POSSIBLE STYLE	

Connecting with others

When you interact with someone, pay attention to their energy and to your response. Do you feel in sync with them or disconnected? If you feel disconnected, you might need to adapt your style to build rapport. Remember that you can choose to 'go into' a different energy. Starting a new interaction in a neutral energy gives you the choice of going up or down a gear, depending on your perceptions of the other person. You can shift towards an initiating style by picking up the pace of your speech and movement, or shift towards a responding style by slowing down a little and taking time. This will help to build rapport.

Another way to connect with others is to take their perspective. We naturally see things from our own point of view (first person). But we can change perspective to look at a situation from the other person's point of view (second person). Sometimes it is helpful to look at a situation as if you are an outsider looking in on both of you (third person). Imagine what an observer would see, hear, think or feel about what you are both doing and saying. Taking a third person, 'fly on the wall', perspective is especially useful for dealing with conflict.

Chapters 9–12 look at specific tips for connecting with each style.

What can go wrong between styles

There is lots of scope for things to go wrong between people of different styles. Each decision-making style (Navigator – deliberate, Mobiliser – quick, Energiser – collaborative, Synthesiser – consultative) is potentially stressful for the other three.

- Navigators may get stressed when they don't know what is happening (e.g. when Mobilisers appear to rush ahead with no plan, and Synthesisers and Energisers throw in too many options and ideas). They don't like meetings which are in their view derailed by brainstorming new ideas instead of making decisions, or when they feel they are being steamrollered by other people and not able to get a word in.

- Mobilisers may get stressed when nothing is happening (e.g. when Synthesisers and Energisers explore options and Navigators take time to think about a course of action). In meetings they can feel frustrated when the pace is slow and taking too long, when others go off the point, when they feel out of control or think that the goal is not being reached.

- Energisers may get stressed when people are not involved and enthusiastic (e.g. when Navigators appear to withdraw, Synthesisers are thoughtful and Mobilisers appear not to listen). In meetings they don't want to feel pushed to do something if they have not been part of the decision, and they don't like people being negative about their ideas, nor being passive.

- Synthesisers may get stressed when not given time to decide (e.g. when Energisers create a chaotic atmosphere, Mobilisers push for action and

Navigators push for closure). They don't like meetings where others do a lot of talking and they can't say what they want, or when they feel a decision is rushed without all the implications being considered.

Even differences in energy and physical movement can cause conflict between people of different styles.

> *Joe (Synthesiser) and his teenage son **Joshua** (Mobiliser) were making their way across a busy station concourse, with Joe in the lead. Synthesisers have a tendency to move indirectly from one place to another, taking in information on the way, while Mobilisers move directly to the goal. They became separated and Joe spent a few moments searching for his son when he reached the other side, feeling annoyed that Joshua had not followed him across the concourse. But Joshua had taken the most direct route and was waiting impatiently for his father, feeling annoyed at the meandering path his father had taken.*

Chapters 9–12 cover conflicts and tensions that can occur between specific styles when their negative emotions are triggered by each other's behaviour. There are also some potential conflicts that apply to all styles due to their underlying preferences. These are covered below.

Conflicts between preferences

Responding or initiating: Having control over the physical environment and how we manage time is influenced by our preferences for responding or initiating. What works for you may not work for your colleague or family member.

Responding styles prefer...	Initiating styles prefer...
Uncluttered space for a calm atmosphere	Busy environment for a stimulating atmosphere
Enough time working alone	Enough time working with other people
Few interruptions and distractions	Some interruptions and distractions
Communicating in writing by emails or reports	Communicating verbally by phone or face to face
Opportunity to think about issues	Opportunity to discuss issues with others
Time to plan before meetings with others	Opportunity to act quickly and move rapidly from one thing to another
Time to reflect after meetings	

> **How does your preference have an impact on your colleagues or family?**

Directing or informing: Whether we communicate in a 'tell' or 'suggest' style can also lead to conflict.

Directing styles...	Informing styles...
Give direction and expect the other person to follow it, but someone with the informing preference may want more explanation	Give information and expect the other person to take it into account before acting, but someone with the directing preference may prefer a clear instruction
May be seen as too direct, especially by someone with the informing preference	May be seen as indecisive, especially by someone with the directing preference
May experience the informing style as manipulative	May experience the directing style as autocratic
If you have a directing preference, bear in mind that your informing colleague may be stressed by being told what to do – they want explanation and information, not just the bare bones of a decision	If you have an informing preference, bear in mind that 'less is more' – your directing colleague may not want explanation or information, but prefer you to get straight to the decision

If you have a preference for directing, you can use a **blended** statement (one which combines direction with information) to get commitment: 'Please do the minutes, as we all need to know what's agreed.'

If you have an informing preference, and need to get someone to do something, you can use a **blended** statement (one which combines information with direction) to ensure that they know what you want done: 'We need to know what's agreed, so please do the minutes.'

> **How does your preference have an impact on your colleagues or family?**

Dealing with conflict

When we feel under threat, the more primitive part of the brain, the amygdala, reacts with a flight or fight response, before the more rational pre-frontal cortex has had time to kick in. Conflict can quickly escalate from minor misunderstandings to a full-blown argument. Here are some general tips on dealing with conflict that apply to all styles:

- Repeat the other person's point of view in your own words, asking questions to clarify their position if needed. This acknowledges the other person, checks you have heard correctly, and gives you time to think.

- Pause after paraphrasing before you state your point of view. Use 'and' not 'but' to bridge to your point of view – 'but' negates what has gone before while 'and' puts the two points of view alongside instead of opposite to each other (compare the impact of replying 'Yes, but...' with 'Yes, and...').

- Avoid 'never' and 'always' when you are describing someone else's behaviour, as this is likely to lead to an emotional reaction and escalation of conflict. It is also factually unlikely that they never or always do something.

- Avoid 'should' and 'ought' as most people don't like being told what to do.

- Avoid phrases like 'with respect' and 'I hear what you say, but...' as these are big red flags that you are about to disagree with them.

- Whenever you can find common ground make it clear that you agree.

- Don't state objections – instead, ask for clarification, seek ideas and make suggestions.

- Switch from the past or present tense to the future – what are we going to do, how can we stop this happening again? This helps to take anger out of the disagreement.[2]

- Consider the problem from their perspective – put yourself in their shoes, rather than sticking firmly in your own.

What can go well between styles

Each style has an underlying preference in common with each of the other three styles and this can provide synergy when there is conflict between them:

- Mobilisers and Energisers share the initiating preference.

- Navigators and Synthesisers share the responding preference.

- Navigators and Mobilisers share the directing preference.

- Energisers and Synthesisers share the informing preference.

- Energisers and Navigators share the process focus.

- Synthesisers and Mobilisers share the outcome focus.

The preferences they share can create common ground and understanding on which to build a stronger connection.

Behaving in a way that mirrors the energy of the other person and that shows you respect their inner drives creates connection. Behaviours that can trigger positive emotions for each style, including what to say to them, are covered in Chapters 9–12.

In Chapters 4–7 we saw that behaviour in our interactions with others is in part driven by our need for self-worth. We have an emotional attachment to our core drives and beliefs, and when we feel that our core drives are not being valued we experience this as a threat to our self-worth and respond in ways that may lead to conflict. Knowing about the styles helps us appreciate the positive motivation and good intentions that are driving someone else's behaviour, even when the impact on us feels negative. Refer back to the table in Chapter 3 (Table 3 in the Appendix) for a reminder of the inner drives and beliefs of people with the different styles.

We judge people by their external behaviour, we guess what their intention is, and there is often a mismatch between the intention of behaviour and the impact it has on others. This is where feedback is useful, so that we can check whether the impact we had on the other person is what we intended, and if it wasn't, then we can take the opportunity to adjust. We tend to judge ourselves on our intentions (good), while we judge others on their impact (bad).

There is also potential synergy between all the styles when they work effectively together. Each style brings something important to the team at work or to family and friends at home. Mobilisers and Synthesisers bring a focus on the outcome or task, Energisers bring a focus on the process for involving people, and Navigators bring a focus on the process for planning how to achieve the task. These are the ingredients for a high performing team (or a happy family).

An important skill in working with others is to act in a way that helps them maintain their self-esteem and their sense of self-worth.

Think of someone you interact with at work or outside work.

What does their physical and verbal behaviour tell you about their likely style?

What might their inner drives and beliefs be?

Where are the potential conflicts with your style and drives?

How could you adapt your approach to meet their needs?

Taking the time to acknowledge the other person's perspective, to respond to what is driving their behaviour and to show that you appreciate their contribution is a key step in building a positive relationship with them.

Specific tips for living and working with each style follow in Chapters 9–12.

Chapter 9

Living and working with Navigators

Picking up physical and verbal cues helps us make more accurate inferences about what the other person is thinking and feeling so we can choose our response more appropriately and respond skilfully to help them fulfil their drives and meet their needs.

This chapter gives some hints and tips on how to adapt to and connect with someone who has the navigator style. Here is a reminder of their key characteristics.

| **Responding role** **Directing communication** **Process focus**  | People with the navigator style *push for a course of action:*
• They tend to move in a deliberate way, speak with a measured tone and pace, and appear calm and **focused.**
• They create a course of action to achieve the **desired result.**
• They make **deliberate** decisions, checking against a thought-through process.
• It tends to come naturally to them to plan, monitor, guide and adjust.
• They keep the group on track and help to anticipate problems.
• They may become stressed when they don't know what is going to happen (or if a plan changes, until they get a new course of action), or if they don't see progress. |

Building rapport

Building rapport is the first step in creating a relationship with another person and often we do it unconsciously. It is easier to build rapport with people who are similar to us, so when someone has a different style from yours, you can build rapport by flexing your style to adapt to theirs.

When communicating with Navigators, you can:

• Be calm, direct and matter of fact

• Stay focused, and not get side-tracked

- Slow down and listen

- Emphasise key milestones

- Talk about the goal and moving towards it

- Think things through – don't just jump in.

Remember, they want to have a course of action to get to the desired result.

During the rapport-building stage, we unconsciously pick up cues from the other person and start to sense whether we like someone or not and how comfortable we are with them. The table below shows how someone with the navigator style might come across to you and what the potential impact on your thoughts and feelings might be.

How Navigators might come across	Their potential impact
Intense and serious	You feel reluctant to approach them
Slow to respond	You feel uncomfortable
Over-focussed on details and process	You wonder what they are withholding
Too directive	You believe they are uncooperative
Not engaged with the team	You feel frustrated by their process and detail focus
Holding back and lacking enthusiasm	
Rigid by imposing structure and process	You dislike being told what to do
Not willing to consider all options	

Clearly, the potentially negative impact on you will influence how you respond and can lead to a cycle of unproductive behaviour from both of you and an escalation of difficulties. We tend to make inferences and fill in the gaps about other people's behaviour. If these inferences are wrong, then we may respond in inappropriate ways and the situation can quickly escalate from a misunderstanding into conflict.

Remaining open-minded and non-judgemental about the other person opens up the channels of communication. Responding in a

calm and measured way will help you to get on to their wavelength, and as the interaction progresses it gives you a chance to understand the positive intentions behind their external behaviour.

Adapting your behaviour to connect

The table below shows the inner drives of Navigators and the dos and don'ts of adapting to them for the three other styles.

How Navigators behave	How to shift towards them
Show **focused** energy	Be calm, direct and matter of fact
Aim to get a **desired** result	Slow down, pause and listen, with intermittent eye contact
Are driven by a pressing need to **anticipate** obstacles	Give them time to express themselves
Believe it is worth the **effort** to think ahead and reach the goal	Stay focused, don't get side-tracked
Make **deliberate** decisions	Be patient as they express their thoughts
Want to keep the group on track and help to anticipate problems	Don't invade their space
Are motivated to think ahead	Don't expect or make small talk
May be stressed when they don't know what is likely to happen or they don't see progress	Let them know of changes to the plan
	Emphasise key milestones
	Talk about the goal and movement towards it
	Encourage them to disclose their thinking and details
	Think things through – don't jump in
	Tell them what is going to happen
	Acknowledge their need for a course of action
	Recognise their contribution to the team

Navigators tend to experience stress when they don't know what is likely to happen (when Mobilisers appear to be rushing ahead with no plan, and Synthesisers and Energisers throw in too many options and ideas). So, if you have one of the other styles, be aware of how your behaviour might impact your navigator colleague.

So when they are stressed, be calm and direct, let them know what to expect, update them on progress and be patient as they express their thoughts.

George had the navigator style and worked in a functional role, supporting an operational team whose leader had the mobiliser style. He was frequently in meetings where issues were discussed and decisions made quickly before he had formulated his thoughts. He felt continually under pressure in these meetings where the operational leaders wanted quick answers and decisions to engineering problems. He was not able to respond quickly as he preferred to think things through before recommending a course of action. He often felt the decisions made were the wrong ones.

He learned that this is a common problem for people with his style: he recognised that he took too long to think, that he needed to use a faster pace and he took the advice to speak up before he had fully formed his thoughts. While this felt uncomfortable at first, he found that his colleagues listened to him and his confidence in expressing his views grew with the positive results.

In this case, George did all the adapting by changing his own style. He would have been even more effective if his colleagues had recognised his need for time and space to think before giving an answer.

What might you need to do differently to relate better to your colleague?

Conflicts and tensions with the other styles

Sometimes the behaviour of people with the other styles can trigger negative emotions in Navigators. It is worth being aware of the behaviours that can trigger negative reactions so that you can avoid them. Typical triggers are shown below.

Responding **Directing** **Process focus**	People being overbearing or intrusive
	People not doing what they're accountable for
	Being given information without a clear purpose
	Fast pace with insufficient time to think
	People being indecisive
	Changes to the plan
	People not following the agreed course of action
	Not knowing what's going to happen

The triggers are activated when Navigators can't fulfil their drives and when their preferences are not valued by others. There are some simple steps people of the other styles can take to avoid triggering their negative reactions.

Trigger	How to adapt and connect
People being overbearing or intrusive	Navigators may find the mobiliser and energiser styles, with their tendency to speak first then think, as overbearing or intrusive. Allow some space for thinking, tone down the volume of your speech, ask them what they think and listen to the answers.
People not doing what they're accountable for	People with the directing preference can be stressed when others don't do what's expected or asked of them. So, when working with Navigators, respond clearly to their requests, so they know where they stand – don't leave them wondering what is happening. Do what you said you were going to do, and if that changes, let them know straightaway.

Being given information without a clear purpose	Energisers and Synthesisers both have the informing preference and may tend to give too much information and detail, or want to involve too many people for the Navigators. Link the information you are providing to the plan or goal and be brief.
Fast pace with insufficient time to think	Mobilisers and Energisers tend to speak and move quickly and Navigators may experience this as pressure to rush without enough thought. Slow down your speech, include pauses and leave some silence. If necessary, arrange to finish the discussion later, after they have had time to consider.
People being indecisive	Synthesisers and Energisers, with the informing preference, may appear indecisive which is unsettling for Navigators, who tend to like clarity and prefer a directing style. Make it clear that you are still evaluating options and let them know when you will make a decision. Navigators also prefer to stick to decisions once made, while Synthesisers and Energisers are comfortable changing decisions in the light of new information. This is best avoided if you want to get on with your navigator colleague.
Changes to the plan	Navigators like to follow the plan but they can be flexible, provided that when there is a change, a new course of action is put in place. Therefore, it is worth taking time to work out a new plan with them.
People not following the agreed course of action	None of the other three styles places as much importance on this as some Navigators. This makes them push harder for the process to be followed and they can appear inflexible, so the other styles need to make allowances for this and not over-react to it.
Not knowing what's going to happen	Navigators can feel stressed when Mobilisers rush ahead to act without a plan or Synthesisers and Energisers generate too many options and involve too many people. Acknowledge their need for a course of action and tell them what's going to happen.

People with the navigator style believe it is worth making the effort to anticipate what might happen. **Tom** *was a manager in a water utility company whose colleague, Hamid, managed the adjacent area and they needed to follow common processes and approaches across the whole region. Tom took an organised, structured approach, valued processes and liked to proceed step by step. He experienced a constant clash of style and approach with Hamid, who was good at dealing with a crisis, liked immediate action and was impatient with processes. Tom was seen by Hamid as pedantic, process-driven, and rule-bound, while Hamid was seen by Tom as unreliable, not to be trusted, and flying by the seat of his pants.*

There were constant problems in the team and their relationship had become so poor, that they could only see the negative side of each other, not the underlying talents. Learning about the styles was the starting point for them to recognise the talents that each brought to the wider team. They also recognised there were opportunities to work together to get the benefits of both styles for the region.

If you live or work with a Navigator, consider how you could adapt your behaviour to avoid triggering their negative emotions.

Triggering positive emotions

Remember that the drive of a Navigator is to *anticipate* and push for a course of action, and that they may get stressed when they don't know what's going to happen. Your behaviour can trigger their positive emotions and help them to feel good. Here is what some Navigators have said they like to get from others:

- Following a process or a plan and getting there, not going off at a tangent

- People repeating back to show they've understood

- Knowing everyone is on the same track

- Clarity of understanding from everyone

- Deciding with the right information

- Being listened to properly

- People showing appreciation – positive comments, following their process

- People giving time to them

- Being inspired by others – by their actions, ideas, arts, music

Here are some of the things you could say to a Navigator to connect with their inner drives and alleviate their stressors:

- 'Could you think about it and make a plan?'

- 'So what you want me to do is . . .'

- 'What are the next steps?'

- 'Let's look at how we are doing against the plan.'

- 'What are the potential problems and what can we do to mitigate them?'

If you live or work with a Navigator, what could you do to trigger their positive emotions?

Ben had the navigator style and found it stressful at weekends when his partner Kate made lots of suggestions about what they might do and there didn't seem to be any clarity about what was going to happen. He found the uncertainty unsettling and this sometimes led to tension between them. They found a way to overcome this problem by discussing and agreeing on a Friday night the plan for the weekend. This removed the stress for Ben and they had happier weekends.

Team contribution

Having a clear sense of the unique contribution of the navigator style is an incentive for people with the other styles to make the effort to adapt and connect with them. Multiple interactions occur in teams, so there are multiple opportunities for misunderstandings, conflict and stress. One way to build a productive climate in a team is to articulate what each person contributes to the team and what they need from their colleagues to help them be effective.

The list below is taken from workshops with managers in a European high technology company. The aim of the workshops was to improve understanding of each other and to create a climate in which people felt they could contribute to their full potential. This is what the participants said about those with the navigator style.

What they bring to the team:

- Measured and thoughtful approach

- Delivered in a calm and measured way

- Progressing to plan/milestones

- Anticipating road blocks and navigating a way round

- Maintaining momentum

- Establishing a process and sticking to it

What they need from the team:

- Time to think

- To be listened to and taken seriously rather than dismissed

- Clear direction and decision on the way forward

- Understanding from others that they like people and not just the process

- Recognition from others that they are flexible and open to change – with an explanation

The public acknowledgement of what the Navigators brought to the team was a major boost to the confidence of the people with this style. They made personal action points afterwards which showed that they felt encouraged to become more involved with the team:

- Get team input and involve others in decision-making.

- Express own view more clearly and often.

> **What can you do to help your navigator colleagues be more effective contributors?**

Chapter **10**

Living and working with Mobilisers

Picking up physical and verbal cues helps us make more accurate inferences about what the other person is thinking and feeling so we can choose our response more appropriately and respond skilfully to help them fulfil their drives and meet their needs.

This chapter gives some hints and tips on how to adapt to and connect with someone who has the mobiliser style. Here is a reminder of their key characteristics.

Initiating role **Directing communication** **Outcome focus** 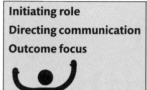	People with the mobiliser style *push for action with results:* <ul><li>They tend to move briskly, speak quite quickly and appear straightforward and **determined.**</li><li>They mobilise resources (including people) to get an **achievable result.**</li><li>They make **quick** decisions with confidence.</li><li>It tends to come naturally to them to decide, direct, mobilise and execute.</li><li>They lead the group to the goal and help to get things accomplished.</li><li>They may get stressed when others do not share their urgency, or nothing is being accomplished or if they feel out of control.</li></ul>

Building rapport

Building rapport is the first step in creating a relationship with another person and often we do it unconsciously. It is easier to build rapport with people who are similar to us, so when someone has a different style from yours, you can build rapport by flexing your style to adapt to theirs.

When communicating with Mobilisers, you can:

- use a fast pace
- be clear
- suggest ideas they haven't considered
- use humour (maybe)

- use a confident tone of voice

- show you are aware of time pressure.

Remember, they want action to get an achievable result.

During the rapport-building stage, we unconsciously pick up cues from the other person and start to sense whether we like them or not and how comfortable we are with them. The table below shows how someone with the mobiliser style might come across to you and what the potential impact on your thoughts and feelings might be.

Mobilisers might come across as	Their potential impact
Bossy and demanding	You feel pressured by the fast pace
Impatient	You feel that they are intrusive
Unaware of other people's feelings	You believe they are autocratic and controlling
Unappreciative of other possible outcomes	You feel frustrated when they rush ahead without taking your views into account
Alienating others by controlling resources	
Not listening to team's ideas	You dislike it when they tell you what to do

Clearly, the potentially negative impact on you will influence how you respond and can lead to a cycle of unproductive behaviour from both of you and an escalation of difficulties. We tend to make inferences and fill in the gaps about other people's behaviour. If these inferences are wrong, then we may respond in inappropriate ways and the situation can quickly escalate from misunderstanding into conflict.

Remaining open-minded and non-judgemental about the other person opens up the channels of communication. Responding in an **active, energetic** way will help you to get on their wavelength and as the interaction progresses, it gives you a chance to understand the positive intentions behind their external behaviour.

Adapting your behaviour to connect

The table below shows the inner drives of Mobilisers and the dos and don'ts of adapting to them for the other three styles.

How Mobilisers behave	How to shift towards them
Show **determined** energy	Be clear and concise – get to the point quickly
Aim to get an **achievable** result	
Are driven by an urgent need to **accomplish** actions	Use a fast pace, strong tone of voice and direct eye contact
Believe it's worth the **risk** to go ahead and act or decide	Show you appreciate the urgency
	Do small talk only when the main issue has been addressed
Want **quick** decisions	
Want to lead the group to the goal and help to get things accomplished	Tell them what you are doing and by when
	Don't talk too much
Are motivated to act or decide	Help them to slow down, stand back and observe
Stressed when nothing is being accomplished or when they feel out of control	Tell them the reasons for things
	Give them specifics
	Suggest ideas they haven't considered
	Push back if necessary, they don't mind
	Join them in their humour

Mobilisers get stressed when nothing is happening (when Synthesisers explore options, Navigators press for a course of action and Energisers talk too much). So, if you have one of the other styles, be aware of how your behaviour might impact your mobiliser colleague.

So when they are stressed, tell them the reasons for things, help them see that something is being done and by when, and join them in their humour.

> **Joseph** often felt frustrated and stressed when his managers didn't do things as quickly as he would have liked. He started to micro-manage them, giving them daily tasks and checking they had done them. But this meant they had little control over their work and did not feel accountable for it – if anything went wrong, it became his fault.
>
> The strategy wasn't working, so Joseph tried a different approach. When he delegated tasks, he gave them the responsibility for deciding how to do it and when it would be done. They learned to keep him informed of progress and he didn't ask about it until the due date. At first, he found this difficult, but gradually he learned to let go and trust them and he had a more motivated team of managers as a result.

What might you need to do differently to relate better to your colleague?

Conflicts and tensions with the other styles

Sometimes the behaviour of people with the other styles can trigger negative emotions in Mobilisers. It is worth being aware of the behaviours that can trigger negative reactions so that you can avoid them. Typical triggers are shown below.

Initiating **Directing** **Outcome focus** 	People being reserved or withholding
	People not doing what they're accountable for
	Being given information without a clear purpose
	Slow pace causing frustration
	People being indecisive
	Nothing being accomplished
	Revisiting earlier discussions or decisions

The triggers are activated when Mobilisers can't fulfil their drives and when their preferences are not valued by others. There are some simple steps people of the other styles can take to avoid triggering their negative reactions.

Trigger	How to adapt and connect
People being reserved or withholding	Mobilisers, with the initiating preference, like to talk things out with others and they think on their feet while they are speaking. But the likely behaviour of Navigators or Synthesisers is to think things through first before speaking. There is a tendency for Mobilisers to think they are deliberately withholding information or effort. When working with Mobilisers, people of the other styles should say what they are thinking, even if their thoughts are not fully formed. The Mobiliser welcomes people expressing their opinions as this signals to them that they are working towards the goals.

(Continued)

Trigger	How to adapt and connect
People not doing what they're accountable for	People with the directing preference can be stressed when others don't do what's expected or asked of them. So, when working with Mobilisers, respond clearly to their requests, so they know where they stand – don't leave them wondering what is happening. They have an urgent need to accomplish things, so if they don't know what is happening, they get frustrated. Do what you said you were going to do, and if that changes, let them know straightaway.
Being given information without a clear purpose	Energisers and Synthesisers both have the informing preference and may tend to give too much information and detail, or want to involve too many people for the Mobiliser. Link the information you are providing to the goal and be brief. Avoid appearing as though you are prevaricating or delaying unnecessarily. Mobilisers do not require too much explanation – they prefer you to get to the point, and if they want to know your reasoning, they will ask for it.
Slow pace causing frustration	Navigators and Synthesisers tend to speak in a measured or patient way and their gestures and body language are more contained and less assertive than those of the Mobilisers. There is a mismatch with the Mobiliser's high-energy approach. Speeding up your speech, speaking more loudly and showing more animated body language will all help to connect with the mobiliser energy. The challenge for Energisers (who naturally display energy) is to be brief and specific – use fewer words and give less explanation than you would like. People of all styles could show that they recognise the Mobiliser's urgency to get things done.
People being indecisive	Synthesisers and Energisers, with the informing preference, like to consult or involve others and take other views and information into account. This process can be time-consuming and leads to decisions taking longer, which is stressful for Mobilisers as they like decisions to be made quickly, so they can get on with doing something. Let them know when you will make a decision and agree the deadline with them, so it is not open-ended – and make sure you get back to them by the deadline.

Nothing being accomplished	Mobilisers have an urgent need to get things done and get stressed when they think nothing is being achieved. They are keen to get on with action and work out the details later. This can cause conflict with Synthesisers and Energisers who like to take time to consult or involve people. It's the same with Navigators who prefer to take time up front to plan in advance and make sure all risks are covered. Acknowledge the Mobiliser's need to get things done and tell them who is doing what. Reassure them that things are happening, and encourage them to take some time out to focus on something else while work is in progress.
Revisiting earlier discussions or decisions	Mobilisers find it very stressful when decisions and discussions are revisited. But for Synthesisers and Energisers, this is a natural consequence of more information becoming available or of more people being involved – which they see as a good thing. Mobilisers can become over-assertive and appear bossy and demanding, so the other styles need to make allowances for this and not over-react to it. Sometimes they may check out and withdraw from the discussion. If they do, the other styles can help by taking steps to involve them again.

People with the mobiliser style believe it is worth taking a risk to act or decide and correcting later. James (who had the mobiliser style) was a manager in a manufacturing plant. There were some issues with the quality of the finished product that urgently needed to be resolved. He wanted the advice of the quality engineer, and demanded an immediate answer to resolve the problem. The quality engineer, with the navigator style, wanted time to investigate and think. James found this extremely frustrating – he wanted immediate action. He pushed for a solution and forced through an action which was not the optimal one and led to further problems later on. However, James still felt that doing something, then tweaking it later, was better than waiting. The quality engineer could have influenced him to wait before acting, if he had shown a sense of urgency and told him that he would work on a solution immediately.

If you live or work with someone with the mobiliser style, consider how you could adapt your behaviour to avoid triggering their negative emotions.

Triggering positive emotions

Remember that the drive of a Mobiliser is to *accomplish* and push for action with results, and that they may get stressed when they feel that nothing is being accomplished. Your behaviour can trigger their positive emotions and help them to feel good. Here is what some Mobilisers have said they like from others:

- Seeing movement towards the target.

- Hearing people say what they are doing.

- People speaking about the task, even if they disagree with them or each other.

- Sense of urgency, getting on with the job without too much discussion.

- Feeling of everyone 'mucking in'.

Here are some of the things you could say to a Mobiliser to connect with their inner drives and alleviate their stressors:

- 'I'll get on to that straightaway.'

- 'This is what I'm going to do...'

- 'I'm sure we can get that done today.'

- 'I'll ask the others to help.'

- 'I've finished it.'

> If you live or work with a Mobiliser, what could you do to trigger their positive emotions?

> **Davina** (who had the mobiliser style) decided to organise a weekend reunion of a group of friends who lived in different parts of the country. She took control, contacted everyone, suggested dates, co-ordinated all the responses, fixed the date and asked the others to volunteer food, drink and activities. They all responded quickly and agreed to take responsibility for various tasks. This made her feel good and they had a great weekend.

Team contribution

Having a clear sense of the unique contribution of people with the mobiliser style is an incentive for the other styles to make the effort to adapt and connect with them. Multiple interactions occur in teams, so there are multiple opportunities for misunderstandings, conflict and stress. One way to build a productive climate in a team is to articulate what each person contributes to the team and what they need from their colleagues to help them be effective.

The list below is taken from workshops with managers in a European high technology company. The aim of the workshops was to improve understanding of each other and to create a climate in which people felt they could contribute to their full potential. This is what the participants said about those with the mobiliser style.

What they bring to the team:

- Action and energy to get on with the task

- Delivering on time

- Leading the group/activity

- Giving structure, clarity, direction

- Taking responsibility for risks and decisions

- Unblocking things, overcoming obstacles

What they need from the team:

- Get to the point quickly – use facts and concrete examples

- Speak up, tell us to stop or if we are unrealistic, tell us why

- Provide useful and meaningful updates – don't keep us in the dark

- Help us prioritise

- Help us step back and reflect

The personal actions identified by people with the mobiliser style were aimed at creating time and space in their single-minded focus to get things done, and for the other styles to make their unique and valuable contributions. They said they needed to:

- step back and reflect more

- be less confrontational

- draw on information and input from others

> **What can you do to help your mobiliser colleagues be more effective contributors?**

Chapter **11**

Living and working with Energisers

Picking up physical and verbal cues helps us make more accurate inferences about what the other person is thinking and feeling so we can choose our response more appropriately and respond skilfully to help them fulfil their drives and meet their needs.

This chapter gives some hints and tips on how to adapt to and connect with someone who has the energiser style. Here is a reminder of their key characteristics.

Initiating role **Informing communication** **Process focus** 	People with the energiser style *push for involvement:* • They tend to move and speak quite quickly and expressively and appear enthusiastic and **engaging.** • They engage others to get an **embraced result.** • They make **collaborative** decisions to ensure buy-in. • It tends to come naturally to them to persuade, energise, facilitate and brainstorm. • They facilitate the group's process and help to raise commitment. • They get stressed when they or others are not involved in what's going on, or if they don't feel accepted.

Building rapport

Building rapport is the first step in creating a relationship with another person and often we do it unconsciously. It is easier to build rapport with people who are similar to us, so when someone has a different style from yours, you can build rapport by flexing your style to adapt to theirs.

When communicating with Energisers, you can:

- listen and show interest
- make positive comments
- highlight the benefits of some options

- give options without direction

- use an upbeat tone of voice

- use personal examples (if appropriate)

- put a positive spin on your ideas.

Remember, they like to involve others and be involved.

During the rapport building stage, we unconsciously pick up cues from the other person and start to sense whether we like someone or not and how comfortable we are with them. The table below shows how Energisers might come across to you and what the potential impact on your thoughts and feelings might be.

How Energisers might come across	Their potential impact
Overly optimistic	You feel pressured by the fast pace
Lacking focus on the task	You feel that they are intrusive
Too talkative	You believe they are attention-seeking
Easily discouraged	
Not mindful of the details or the need for structure and planning	You feel stressed by the chaotic atmosphere
Frenetic by wanting to involve and enthuse others	You dislike it when they don't do what you've asked
Throwing in too many ideas	

Clearly, the potentially negative impact on you of the energiser style will influence how you respond and can lead to a cycle of unproductive behaviour from both of you and an escalation of difficulties. We tend to make inferences and fill in the gaps about other people's behaviour. If these inferences are wrong, then we may respond in inappropriate ways and the situation can quickly escalate from misunderstanding into conflict.

Remaining open-minded and non-judgemental about the other person opens up the channels of communication. Responding to the Energiser in an **encouraging and animated** way will help you to get on their wavelength, and as the interaction progresses it gives you a chance to understand the positive intentions behind their external behaviour.

Adapting your behaviour to connect

The table below shows the inner drives of Energisers and the dos and don'ts of adapting to them for the other three styles.

How Energisers behave	How to shift towards them
Show **engaging** energy	Start with small talk
Aim to get an **embraced** result	Use a fast pace, be animated and expressive in body language
Are driven by an urgent need to **involve** others and be involved	Listen as they talk things through and show interest
Believe it is worth the **energy** spent to involve everyone and get them to want to...	Appear open and show enthusiasm
Want **collaborative** decisions	Reinforce ideas with positive comments
Want to facilitate the group's process and help to raise commitment	Give information in an upbeat tone of voice
Are motivated to include everyone	Use personal examples
	Highlight the benefits of some options
May be stressed when they are not involved in what's going on	Put a positive spin on your ideas
	Act as a sounding board for them to help them think things through

Energisers get stressed when people are not involved and enthusiastic (when Navigators and Synthesisers are quiet and Mobilisers appear not to listen to their ideas). So, if you have one of the other styles, be aware of how your behaviour might impact your energiser colleague.

So when they are stressed, listen as they talk things out, encourage their active participation and express your ideas, thoughts and feelings.

> At work people with the energiser style have the potential to contribute by engaging others to participate, but a pitfall may be creating a chaotic atmosphere. Lizzie had the energiser style and worked in an open-plan office, though she also spent half her time at other locations. Her colleagues always knew when she was in the office as she spoke loudly, engaged with others and whenever she had an idea, she was compelled to discuss it straightaway. Her enthusiasm was infectious but a downside for colleagues was that they were distracted from their own work. To minimise disruption to others, one of her colleagues agreed to act as her sounding board and they arranged their meetings in a room away from the others.

Some people with this style describe themselves as 'bossy' – more usually a descriptor of the mobiliser style. Although they see themselves as bossy, other people do not see them in the same way. It is perhaps their willingness and ability to bring people together and to organise things for other people to enjoy, that can make them feel bossy. Sometimes people with an informing style of communication (Energisers and Synthesisers) can be perceived as bossy when they use directing language, as it does not come naturally to them.

> **What might you need to do differently to relate better to your colleague?**

Conflicts and tensions with the other styles

Sometimes the behaviour of people with the other styles can trigger negative emotions in Energisers. It is worth being aware of the behaviours that can trigger negative reactions so that you can avoid them. Typical triggers are shown below.

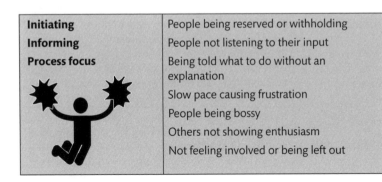

Initiating Informing Process focus	People being reserved or withholding
	People not listening to their input
	Being told what to do without an explanation
	Slow pace causing frustration
	People being bossy
	Others not showing enthusiasm
	Not feeling involved or being left out

The triggers are activated when Energisers can't fulfil their drives and when their preferences are not valued by others. There are some simple steps people of the other styles can take to avoid triggering their negative reactions.

Trigger	How to adapt and connect
People being reserved or withholding	Energisers may see the navigator and synthesiser styles, with their tendency to think first then (maybe) speak as reserved and they may believe the others are withholding information or commitment. Respond promptly, ideally with some positive remarks, even if you haven't fully thought them through. For Energisers it is better if you say anything rather than nothing. If you have the mobiliser style, listen to their ideas and avoid criticising them.
People not listening to their input	Energisers, with the informing and initiating preferences, like to involve others in discussion and explain and explore their ideas. They can be stressed when others aren't willing to engage with them. Take some time to listen to their ideas and discuss them, even if it means breaking off from your own activities for a short time.
Being told what to do without an explanation	Mobilisers and Navigators both have the directing preference and may tend to give instruction with little explanation. This is stressful for Energisers, so make an effort to give information or explanation as this will help them feel committed to what you want them to do. Synthesisers will naturally provide information, but may not be sufficiently clear on what specifically they want done.
Slow pace causing frustration	Navigators and Synthesisers tend to speak and move in a sustained and thoughtful manner, and Energisers may feel frustrated by the slower pace. Energisers tend to fill any silence, which further decreases the opportunity for the others to respond. Avoid pausing, speed up your speech and vary your tone of voice. If necessary, tell them you need some time to think about it and leave them with some encouraging remarks.
People being bossy	Energisers naturally like to discuss ideas and options. Therefore, when communicating with them, take the time to inform and explain. Mobilisers and Navigators should avoid appearing to instruct or to close down options that the Energisers may feel are worth considering.

Others not showing enthusiasm	Energisers have the most expressive and animated style and they may interpret the less effusive style of Navigators and Synthesisers as a lack of enthusiasm. When talking to Energisers, tell them what you are thinking, speed up your pace and use more expressive gestures.
Not feeling involved or being left out	The core inner driver of Energisers is to involve others to get a result that is embraced by everyone. They like to be involved themselves and may become demotivated if they feel excluded from activities. Ensure that you involve Energisers or at least keep them informed so they know what's going on.

*Energisers tend to have plenty to say and others may find this overpowering or frustrating, especially when they feel they can't get heard themselves. This was the case with **Paul**, who had the synthesiser style. On one occasion he said to his energiser colleague Sally, 'The more fuss you make, the less seriously I take you.' He learned that he sometimes needed to butt in, which felt rude, but it was the only way to make sure his points were considered.*

If you live or work with an Energiser, consider how you could adapt your behaviour to avoid triggering their negative emotions.

Triggering their positive emotions

Remember that the drive of an Energiser is to *involve* and that they may get stressed when they or others are not involved. Your behaviour can trigger their positive emotions and help them to feel good. Here is what some Energisers have said they like to get from others:

- Seeing the group using their energy and seeing where it takes them.

- Sense of optimism – 'we' can do this.

- People responding openly and honestly.

- The whole group feeling important, not only individuals.

- People being open and curious.

- People showing positive emotions.

- People looking engaged and interested.

Here are some of the things you could say to an Energiser to connect with their inner drive and alleviate their stressors:

- 'I'd love to work with you on that.'

- 'That's a really good idea.'

- 'When can we start?'

- 'How about inviting the others?'

- 'What does everyone think about that?'

> **If you live or work with an Energiser, what could you do to trigger their positive emotions?**

A group of friends had been talking about a weekend away to Barcelona but no one had done anything about it. In the group, there were three with the energiser style, two with navigator and two with synthesiser. If there had been someone with the mobiliser style ('Let's get it done now!'), it is likely that the date would have been agreed and flights and hotel already booked. Time went on and eventually, Ellie (an Energiser) invited everyone to her house ('Let's get started') for a discussion and social get-together. Everyone responded with enthusiasm and she felt good that she had got the trip off the ground. The people with the synthesiser style brought along information about Barcelona and got busy on the internet, exploring options for flights and accommodation ('What result do we need'?) so that the best decisions could be made. And the two Navigators started to work out a programme for the weekend ('What's the plan?').

Clearly, having a particular style does not mean you have to take on tasks associated with that style, nor that you need a particular style in order to complete a particular task successfully. But it demonstrates that we naturally tend to focus first on the things that are important to us and that draw on our unique strengths.

Team contribution

Having a clear sense of the unique contribution of people with the energiser style is an incentive for the other styles to make the effort to adapt and connect with them. Multiple interactions occur in teams, so there are multiple opportunities for misunderstandings, conflict and stress. One way to build a productive climate in a team is to articulate what each person contributes to the team and what they need from their colleagues to help them be effective.

The list below is taken from workshops with managers in a European high technology company. The aim of the workshops was to improve understanding of each other and to create a climate in which people felt they could contribute to their full potential. This is what the participants said about those with the energiser style.

What they bring to the team:

- Fun, enjoyment, collaboration and encouragement

- Enthusiasm, energy and involving others

- Social 'glue' not just task, connections to others

- Bring together different views and positions

- Move on – speed of ideas

- Positive spin and optimistic

- Enable others to discover new things

- Network with others – natural desire to share

What they need from the team:

- To be involved and engaged early

- Others not being negative

- Others being genuine and honest

- Asking how they are in a genuine way

- Direction but not too much

- Response – tell us how you feel

- Don't be non-committal – say it, mean it, inside and outside the meeting

During the workshop someone had the idea of setting up a peer-to-peer coaching network to continue to learn how to adapt their behaviour to each other and enable the individual strengths of all team members to flourish within the group. Not surprisingly, it was two of the Energisers who took the action to implement this idea.

Other personal actions identified by the Energisers included:

- Give direction rather than information.

- Be explicit about what I want from my team.

One participant said: 'I've noticed I need to be more specific and focused, which is not a bad thing.'

What can you do to help your energiser colleagues to be more effective contributors?

Chapter **12**

Living and working with Synthesisers

Picking up physical and verbal cues helps us make more accurate inferences about what the other person is thinking and feeling so we can choose our response more appropriately and respond skilfully to help them fulfil their drives and meet their needs.

This chapter gives some hints and tips on how to adapt to and connect with someone who has the synthesiser style. Here is a reminder of their key characteristics.

Responding role **Informing communication** **Outcome focus** 	People with the synthesiser style *push for the best result:* • They tend to move and speak in an unassuming way, and appear patient and **approachable.** • They gather information and input to get the **best result.** • They make **consultative** decisions, integrating many sources of input and points of view. • It tends to come naturally to them to define, clarify, support and integrate. • They support the group's process and help to avoid mistakes. • They may get stressed when they don't have enough time or are not given credit for their efforts, or if they are pressed to decide too quickly.

Building rapport

Building rapport is the first step in creating a relationship with another person and often we do it unconsciously. It is easier to build rapport with people who are similar to us, so when someone has a different style from yours, you can build rapport by flexing your style to adapt to theirs.

When communicating with Synthesisers, you can:

• be open and unassuming

• allow pauses for thinking time

- ask questions and listen to the answers

- don't pressure them to make decisions

- offer choices and pros and cons

- ask them where they are in their thoughts

- give them time to process information.

Remember, they want information and input so they can get the best result.

During the rapport-building stage, we unconsciously pick up cues from the other person and start to sense whether we like someone or not and how comfortable we are with them. The table below shows how Synthesisers might come across to you and what the potential impact on your thoughts and feelings might be.

How Synthesisers might come across	Their potential impact
Unassertive	You feel impatient with the slow pace
Going into too much depth	
Taking too much time and meandering around the topic	You feel uncomfortable with pauses
	You wonder what they are thinking
Lacking clarity of direction	You believe they are submissive
Being slow to decide and to act	You feel frustrated when they consult you but then appear to ignore your views
Subservient by accommodating too many needs	
Making things too complicated	You dislike it when they don't do what you've asked

Clearly, the potentially negative impact on you of the synthesiser style will influence how you respond and can lead to a cycle of unproductive behaviour from both of you and an escalation of difficulties. We tend to make inferences and fill in the gaps about other people's behaviour. If these inferences are wrong, then we may respond in inappropriate ways and the situation can quickly escalate from misunderstanding into conflict.

Remaining open-minded and non-judgemental about the other person opens up the channels of communication. Responding to the Synthesiser in a **friendly and patient** way will help you to get on their wavelength, and as the interaction progresses it gives you a chance to understand the positive intentions behind their behaviour.

Adapting your behaviour to connect

The table below shows the inner drives of Synthesisers and the dos and don'ts of adapting to them for the other three styles.

How Synthesisers behave	How to shift towards them
Show **approachable** energy	Be open and friendly but not too expressive
Aim to get the **best result** possible	Make eye contact and use a softer voice, be more low key
Are driven by a pressing need to **integrate** input	
Believe it's worth the **time** it takes to integrate and reconcile many inputs	Allow pauses for thinking time
	Listen to them without interruption
	Ask questions and listen carefully to the answers
Want **consultative** decisions	Give them time to reflect and integrate
Want to support the group's process and help avoid mistakes	Ask them where they are in their thoughts
Are motivated to reconcile everything	Don't pressure them to make a decision immediately
May be stressed when they are not given enough time or credit or are pressed to decide too quickly	Offer choices and pros and cons
	Give them credit for their input
	Tell them what you need from them

Synthesisers tend to experience stress when they are not given time to decide or not given credit for their contribution (when Mobilisers charge ahead, Energisers talk too much and Navigators press for a course of action). So, if you have one of the other styles, be aware of how your behaviour might impact your synthesiser colleague.

So when they are stressed, be friendly but not too expressive, patiently provide information and encouragement and give them time to reflect and integrate.

> *Katie* (Synthesiser) and her partner Billy (Navigator) were moving abroad
> with Billy's work. He had gone ahead, while Katie was due to move with the
> children at the end of the school term. Katie wanted to keep her job for as
> long as possible and had not decided when to hand in her notice. She felt
> pressurised by Billy, who every time they spoke asked when she was going to
> stop work. He wanted to know what her plan was, while she wanted to put
> off the decision until she had considered all the options and the time felt
> right. This difference between them was resolved by Katie telling Billy the
> latest date she would leave, while she kept her options open by knowing she
> could bring it forward if she wanted to.

What might you need to do differently to relate better to your colleague?

Conflicts and tensions with the other styles

Sometimes the behaviour of people with the other styles can trigger negative emotions in Synthesisers. It is worth being aware of the behaviours that can trigger negative reactions so that you can avoid them. Typical triggers are shown below.

Responding	People being overbearing or intrusive
Informing	People not listening to their input
Outcome focus	Being told what to do without an explanation
	Fast pace with insufficient time to think
	People being bossy
	Not having enough time to integrate all the information
	Not being given credit for their contribution
	Being forced to make a decision before they are ready

The triggers are activated when Synthesisers can't fulfil their drives and when their preferences are not valued by others. There are some simple steps people of the other styles can take to avoid triggering their negative reactions.

Trigger	How to adapt and connect
People being overbearing or intrusive	Synthesisers may experience the mobiliser and energiser styles, with their tendency to speak first then think, as overbearing or intrusive. Allow some space for thinking, tone down the volume of your speech, ask them what they think and listen to the answers.
People not listening to their input	People with the responding preference can be stressed when they cannot get into the conversation to say what they are thinking. You can help them by asking them for their thoughts and giving them the space and time to articulate them.
Being told what to do without an explanation	Navigators and Mobilisers both have the directing preference and may tend to give too much instruction and too little explanation for Synthesisers. While they may appear to agree (because they tend to accommodate to others), they may in practice ignore the instruction, so it is worth taking a little extra time to make sure they are able to express any concerns.
Fast pace with insufficient time to think	Mobilisers and Energisers tend to speak and move quickly and Synthesisers may experience this as pressure to rush without considering all the options. Slow down your speech, include pauses and leave some silence. Be patient. If necessary, arrange to finish the discussion later after they have had time to consider.
People being bossy	Navigators and Mobilisers, with the directing preference, may appear bossy, and this can cause Synthesisers to resist passively. Ask for their opinions and consider their input. Resist the temptation to tell – instead give an explanation and let them have some input.

Not having enough time to integrate all the information	Help them work out how much time they need, and agree timescales with them, so you don't chase them for their input before the agreed date. And if there isn't as much time as they want, help them prioritise and accept that sometimes good enough is ok.
Not being given credit for their contribution	Synthesisers often report that they propose ideas or make suggestions and that other people get the credit for it. Make sure you acknowledge their input and give them feedback on their work.
Being forced to make a decision before they are ready	Synthesisers can feel stressed when Mobilisers rush ahead to act without considering all the options, or Navigators want to work out a course of action, or Energisers create a chaotic atmosphere by involving too many people. Acknowledge their need for time, help them work out what needs to happen for them to make a decision, and agree how long that will take.

People attending a workshop carried out a practical activity in groups with a mixture of styles. When the activity was debriefed, it was clear that the Synthesisers had experienced some of their negative triggers because of the behaviour of people with the other styles, especially the behaviour of the Mobilisers in their group who didn't listen to them and who stood and leaned over the table, rather than sitting around the table with the others. The Synthesisers concluded that it would have helped them with the task if they had been able to work in smaller groups so there was no argument. They felt that the contribution of their style was finding 'the strategy to achieve the task, serving each other and not making a noise' – a quite different approach from their mobiliser colleagues to achieving tasks.

If you live or work with a Synthesiser, consider how you could adapt your behaviour to avoid triggering their negative emotions.

Triggering positive emotions

Remember that the drive of a Synthesiser is to *integrate* and push for the best result and they may get stressed when they don't have enough input, time or credit for their work. Your behaviour can trigger their positive emotions and help them to feel good. Here is what some Synthesisers have said they like to get from others:

- Being allowed the time and space to speak.
- Enabling the outcome to develop and emerge.
- People listening to what they have to contribute.
- Others being comfortable with some silence.
- People acknowledging their contribution.
- Others taking responsibility – a sign of their engagement.
- Others showing care for them.
- People acting as a sounding board.

Here are some of the things you could say to a Synthesiser to connect with their inner drive and alleviate their stressors:

- 'What do you think about this idea?'
- 'How long would you like to finish that report?'
- 'This piece of work is really helpful.'
- 'I like your ideas about that.'
- 'What do you see as the pros and cons?'

If you live or work with a Synthesiser, what could you do to trigger their positive emotions?

> **Chrissie** put together a training course for call centre staff. She drew on material from lots of different sources, as well as talking to a broad range of people about what was needed. She synthesised the information and came up with an innovative design. Her clients were delighted with the course and she was given a lot of praise and recognition for her work. This made her feel that all the effort had been worthwhile, even though her colleagues and clients had no idea how much time she had put into it.

Team contribution

Having a clear sense of the unique contribution of Synthesisers is an incentive for the other styles to make the effort to adapt and connect with them. Multiple interactions occur in teams, so there are multiple opportunities for misunderstandings, conflict and stress. One way to build a productive climate in a team is to articulate what each person contributes to the team and what they need from their colleagues to help them be effective.

The list below is taken from workshops with managers in a European high technology company. The aim of the workshops was to improve understanding of each other and to create a climate in which people felt they could contribute to their full potential. This is what the participants said about Synthesisers.

What they bring to the team:

- Ability to integrate information
- Focus on the outcome – deliver best result
- Consultative style, involving others
- Listening to others
- Flexible, adaptable approach
- Calmness

What they need from the team:

- Patience that we will deliver
- Trust that we will do the best we can

- Support when necessary

- Credit where credit's due

- Recognition that the other three styles always need someone who 'synthesises'!

- Thinking time alone

The public acknowledgement of what the Synthesiser brought to the team was a major boost to the confidence of people with this style. They made personal action points afterwards which showed that they felt encouraged to become more involved with the team:

- Say what I am thinking more often – simply.

- Be more assertive and speak more confidently.

- Push myself forward in discussions on subjects where I am less confident or knowledgeable.

What can you do to help your synthesiser colleagues to be more effective contributors?

Part 3

How to apply
the styles in
your work
and life

Chapter **13**

Strategies for positive influence and impact

Everyone thinks of changing the world but no one thinks of changing himself

Leo Tolstoy

Everything we do or say has an impact on others, whether we intend it or not. Even when other people are not present, we instinctively communicate feelings through our facial expressions. When watching a film or reading a book, we react verbally and physically, even when there is no one present to see or hear us. And if someone is present, what we do or say has some impact on them, and the impact influences how they respond to us.

The impact and how it influences them may not be what we intended. Their interpretation of our behaviour is affected by what is going on in their own minds, and they don't know what is going on in ours. For example, someone had just been given some bad news by their boss, and was feeling upset about it. When a colleague greeted them cheerfully, they responded grumpily, with the result that the colleague felt rebuffed and avoided them for the rest of the day – an outcome that neither of them really wanted.

Having a positive influence and impact is about being able to match your behaviour to your intention, to what you want to achieve. There is often an 'influence gap' between what we **intend** by our words and actions and the **impact** it has on the other person. For example, a person with the mobiliser style intends to get things done quickly. But the impact, if their approach is seen as a 'bull in a china shop', can be that people resist going along with what they want, and they lose their influence.

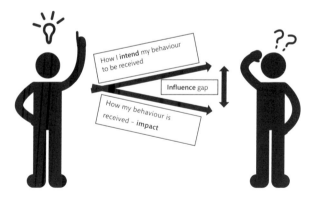

Given that we communicate instinctively most of the time, it makes sense to be aware of what and how we are communicating, so that the impact of our communication matches our intention and we have a positive influence to get better outcomes for everyone.

> **Shanti** was a team leader in a call centre and she had some problems at home. Her unhappiness came across in how she communicated to her staff and the atmosphere in the team changed. The impact of her behaviour had a negative influence on the team and their performance went from being one of the highest to one of the lowest. Eventually, her boss realised there was a problem and moved her temporarily (and sensitively) to a different role until she resolved her domestic problems. The team's performance quickly improved under a new leader.

Communication process

The meaning of a communication is the impact on the listener and their response to your inputs – the words you use and the way you put them across, your voice tone and body language. The messages sent by your words, tone of voice and body language need to be consistent. If they are not, people may pay more attention to what your tone and body language imply, rather than to the words you use.[1]

A useful way to think about communicating with others is as a model of input – process – outcome.

INPUTS	PROCESS	OUTCOMES
Words	Rapport	Impact and intention
Voice tone	Listening	Intended result achieved
Body language	Advocacy	(or not!)
	Inquiry	

Things can go right or wrong at any stage in this process. The impact of our **inputs**, and how we interact during the **process**, can lead to different **outcomes** than we intended. There is a phrase used in neuro-linguistic programming (NLP) that 'every communication has a meaning, whether you want it to or not' and 'the meaning of a communication is the response it gets!'[2]

You have control over large parts of this process – setting the outcome you want, choosing your words, tone of voice and body language, building rapport and managing the balance you take between advocating your own position and inquiring about the other person's position. These will all influence whether you achieve your intended result.

Setting outcomes

Start a communication with the end in mind. For any communication, clarify your desired outcome:

- What do you want to achieve? What do you want to be different as a result of your communication? Why are you communicating?

- How will you know you've achieved it?

- What will you see, hear, think and feel which will tell you that you have achieved it?

It is also worth thinking about what outcomes your audience would like. Put yourself in their shoes and ask yourself:

- What do they want from this interaction?

- What is in it for them?

- What might engage them?

- What would you want to hear if you were in their position?

Even an apparently simple communication can be improved by using this approach. For example, you might decide to call your elderly mother who lives alone 100 miles away. You are probably ringing because you want to make sure she is ok and show that you care about her. During the call, something comes up, you have a slight disagreement and you end the call with both of you feeling dissatisfied. Sound familiar? This was not what you wanted to achieve. Taking a few moments before the call to remind yourself why you are calling, and what your mother might want from the conversation, makes it more likely that you will achieve what you want. Having an intention in mind will shape what you say and how you say it and will lead to a better outcome. Try it next time you make a call like this.

Words

Language needs to be simple, direct and appealing and it is more effective to use active rather than passive forms of speech: 'I will book the train tickets' rather than 'The train tickets will be booked by me.'

Try to appeal to the senses, especially sight, sound and touch, and to the emotions (see the next chapter for more on this). Talk about how you feel, as well as what you think. Use positive language and positive images – describe what you want, rather than what you don't want. For example, if you were going to diet, rather than setting your goal as 'to lose weight', it is more motivating to set your goal as 'to look slim and healthy'. This provides a positive future vision, something that you can move towards, rather than something you are moving away from – focus on the gain rather than the pain.

Tone of voice

Meaning is also carried by the emphasis placed on different words, and the pace of your speech. Depending on where you put the emphasis, the sentence 'I didn't say he stole your money' can have many different meanings. Try it with the emphasis on each word separately in turn.

Think about what the key words are in your message, the words you want people to remember, and make sure you place the emphasis on these words and that they are memorable. Politicians use slogans to simplify their message and these can be very effective. Good communicators can get their message across in a few well-chosen phrases. In news headlines a lot of information is conveyed in few words.

A good communicator will do the following:

- Vary the tone of their voice
- Vary their speed of delivery
- Emphasise key words to give them meaning

- Pause and use silence to focus attention

- Project their voice to the relevant group

- Speak with enthusiasm.

Body language

Be aware of your own body language when you are communicating and the messages it sends.

To project a positive image do the following:

- Adopt a relaxed but alert body posture

- Straighten up (whether sitting or standing)

- Square and lower your shoulders

- Breathe lower into your abdomen rather than high in your chest

- Avoid fiddling with things

- Make eye contact with your audience.

Building rapport

When we want to get on well with someone, whether in work or outside work, we need to build rapport with them. Matching their energy is a good way to start to build rapport, so if they are coming across as animated and energetic, or calm and reserved, then matching their speed and tone of voice, their facial expressions, hand gestures and body posture, is useful (though not so much that they think you are mocking them). Generally, we do this matching and mirroring unconsciously – when you are in rapport with someone, it is likely that you will hold a similar body posture and make similar movements.

Finding some common ground is a good way to build rapport. It might be common interests outside work (sport, children, hobbies) or some agreement about things inside work. It is easier to express disagreement with someone without causing offence when you already have a relationship with them and there are things that you have in common.

Being alert to the reaction of someone to what you have said will show you whether they have received it as you intended. If their reaction surprises or puzzles you, then this is an indication that they have not interpreted your communication in the way you intended.

Building trust

Trust in a relationship usually develops over time. When people trust each other, they are likely to reveal more about their true thoughts and feelings, and this further enhances the degree of trust between them. However, revealing more about yourself in this way is also risky, as the other person might not reciprocate or agree with you.

The figure below shows how the things people are willing to talk about influence the quality of the relationship. Much of our communication is at the lower levels: How are you? Did you see the TV last night? What about the football match? We tend to be cautious about expressing our opinions and ideas (I'm voting for party x, I'd like to see more green energy), and even more reticent about revealing our feelings. As people move from talking about facts and ideas up to revealing more about their own feelings and values, the level of risk increases, but so does the level of trust and commitment. Therefore, if you want to build trust, revealing more about your own feelings and your values and beliefs will encourage people to trust you.

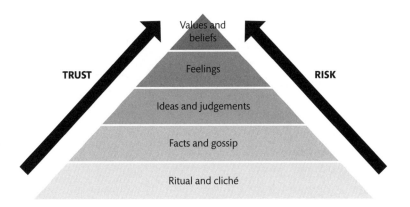

Source: Powell J[3]

Active listening

People can appear to listen by nodding and making eye contact, but their response sometimes tells you that they are not truly listening to what you have said. Truly active listening includes not only giving physical signs that you are listening (making eye contact, nodding and vocalising), but also asking questions, reflecting back and summarising what the other person has said to show you have understood it.

Give and take

We often think that communicating with other people is about telling them what we think, rather than asking them what they think. The economist J K Galbraith[4] summed this up when he said 'In the choice between changing one's mind and proving there's no need to, most people get busy on the proof.' True communication is genuinely two-way, with each person being willing to change their mind. The give and take of communication is known as advocacy (how people make statements) and inquiry (how people ask questions).[5] High quality in both advocacy and inquiry facilitates mutual learning about each other's point of view and a collaborative approach to resolving differences.

The figure below shows the behaviours when people have low levels of give and take (bottom left corner) and high levels (top right corner).

HIGH

Explain their thinking
Give examples
Seek others' views
Probe others' thinking
Share their reasoning
Encourage challenge

State conclusions
Don't give examples
Don't explain their thinking
Seek confirming views
Ask leading questions
Discourage challenge

LOW

Planning what to say

It might seem odd to plan to communicate. After all, we communicate all the time, usually without thinking about it. But that's the problem – often our communication does not achieve the result we want and some advance thought can make a big difference. The template below can be used to plan any type of communication at work or at home (a phone call, a team briefing, a conversation about progress on a project, a meeting, a performance discussion).

What is your desired outcome for this communication? What do you want to be different after the communication?

How will you know you have achieved your desired outcome? What will you see, hear, think and feel? What will others be saying, doing, thinking and feeling?

What will you say? What is your opening statement to engage the audience and describe the topic clearly?

(Continued)

Consider what the audience might want from the communication. What questions or objections might they have? What is their perspective on the issue?

What are the main points you want to get across? How will you communicate them?

What emotion do you want to convey in your tone of voice? What style will convey this?

What facial expression, body posture and tone of voice will be consistent with the message?

What will be a successful ending for the interaction? How will you close?

Sam had to work on a key project with a newly appointed manager in another part of the business, based in the US, so it was not possible to meet face to face and the time overlap of their working days was limited. The American manager was female and this added to Sam's apprehension about the meeting and his worry that he would not be able to influence her to get what he needed. He had set up a virtual meeting with her for the following week but had done no planning for the meeting. We used the template above to talk through his approach.

Prior to our discussion, he had not thought about specifically what he wanted from the meeting or how to go about getting it. He was quiet and reserved, with a navigator style, and did not typically take the initiative in meetings, so we worked on what he would say to open the meeting, including setting out the purpose. He rehearsed this with me, and with feedback about his speed and tone of voice and his body language, he improved it to have a more assertive impact. He also found it helpful to think about what the other manager might want from the meeting and what would be a success from her point of view, and we discussed how to end the meeting on a positive note.

A few weeks later, at our next session, he was delighted to tell me that the meeting had gone very well and he was continuing to use the planning template for other communications.

Positive influence and impact

Each style has a specific focus for how they influence other people and their energy creates an impact on others. Being aware of your strengths in influencing others enhances your confidence and means you can use your talents consciously. Being aware of the pitfalls of each style means you can avoid them in yourself and respond constructively to them in others. The next two tables illustrate the strengths and the pitfalls of each style.

Influencing Strengths

	NAVIGATOR	MOBILISER	ENERGISER	SYNTHESISER
How they influence	Influence by pushing for a course of action	Influence by pushing for action with results	Influence by pushing for involvement	Influence by pushing for the best result
	Focus on defining the process for achieving the goal	Clear focus on the goal or task and removing obstacles	Bring energy and enthusiasm to the task	Bring relevant information and input to the task
	Calm communication style	Straightforward communication style	Persuasive communication style	Patient communication style
	Involve others to ensure the plan stays on track	Build rapport with colleagues around the goal	Encourage and involve others to get buy in	Listen to others and provide support to achieve the goal
Positive impact on others	Create an orderly climate	Create a pace-setting climate	Create an affiliative climate	Create a democratic climate
	Focused energy pushes the team to follow a course of action	Determined energy pushes the team to achieve the task	Engaging energy pulls the team along and encourages co-operation	Approachable energy draws input from the team
	Help to keep projects and teams on track	Help to get things accomplished	Help to raise commitment from others by getting their buy-in	Help to avoid mistakes by gathering as much relevant information as possible

	NAVIGATOR	MOBILISER	ENERGISER	SYNTHESISER
Potential pitfalls	May lose focus on the task, due to over-emphasis on processes and risks	May not achieve the best result, due to not fully exploring options	May lose focus on the task, due to involving too many people	May take too long to achieve the result, due to wanting too much input
	May appear slow or process-driven	May not consider all the possible options and approaches	May spend too much time and energy on getting everyone's input	May consider too many options and approaches
	May appear reluctant to consider other options	May neglect to share information with others	May lose sight of the actions needed to achieve the goal	May add information late in the process
	May appear inflexible in decisions	May take decisions too quickly without getting buy-in	Decisions and action planning may lack clarity	Decision-making process may be unclear to others
Behaviours with potential negative impact on others	May neglect to greet and chat to others	May not listen to colleagues and may ignore their feelings	May talk too much and prevent others giving their views	May appear to ignore input from others making them feel devalued
	May appear uninterested or unenthusiastic when interacting	May not take the time to build rapport	May get discouraged if others do not show enthusiasm	May not be clear about what they want others to do
	May not ask questions of others and this may limit options	May give advice when not needed and appear bossy	May deter colleagues from expressing concerns	May avoid asking challenging questions
	May withdraw when plans are ignored or not supported	May become impatient or aggressive when nothing appears to be happening	May create a chaotic environment when trying to engage others	May be too accommodating and perceived as weak

How can you make sure you maximise your strengths in positive influence and impact while avoiding the potential downsides? What can you do differently?

Chapter 14

Engaging communication

Great leadership works through the emotions

Daniel Goleman[1]

Emotions are part of everything we do. Although we talk about our brains being 'hard-wired' and 'programmed', people are not computers. Our behaviours reflect a complex intertwining of habits, thoughts, feelings, values, beliefs and attitudes. Communication that engages these aspects, and especially our emotions, is much more effective than communication that appeals only to our reason. Think of how an economist might explain facts and figures in a rational way, compared with how a politician uses the same data to elicit an emotional response in the listener.

Engaging communication involves appealing to people's emotions as well as to their rational thought processes. Brian Cox, professor of particle physics at the University of Manchester, is an engaging communicator. He can explain complex concepts and maths equations in a way that connects with audiences, both on TV and live. His 2017 UK tour attracted thousands of people, few of whom understand relativity, but who nevertheless chose to spend their time listening to him speak. This is because he communicates his own emotions, and engages the emotions of his audience, through his choice of words, tone of voice and body language. We are captivated by his sense of awe and enthusiasm and these elicit similar emotions in us.

To connect with others in an engaging way, we need to be aware of our own emotions and able to manage them so that they have the impact we intend. We also need to be aware of how emotions influence the actions and decisions of other people.

In this chapter you will learn how to flex your behaviour in different situations to appeal to people's emotions, inner drives and beliefs, as well as to their rational minds.

Commitment vs compliance

We know that to get commitment from others rather than merely compliance, you need to engage people's emotions. Rational explanation may get compliance (they do it because you have told them to), while an appeal to someone's emotions gets commitment (they do it because they want to). This is why disaster appeals focus on human tragedies and why drink driving campaigns at Christmas show pictures of injured people rather than statistics.

Research[2] has shown that when people are making a decision to buy something, their thinking is 80% logic and 20% emotion, up to the point of purchase. But at the point of purchase, their decision is 80% emotion and 20% logic –

they go with their gut instinct. People choose things for emotional reasons and we often make decisions unconsciously, and then use our conscious mind to rationalise the decision to ourselves. If you have a dog, think about why you chose that particular dog. It is likely that, after weighing up various factors in a rational way, there were emotional factors that propelled you into making the final choice. Similarly, think about the last car you bought – what was it that tipped you at the end of the decision process into that particular choice?

Emotions play an important role in decision-making. Neuroscientists agree that emotions and thinking are 'completely intertwined'[3] and that emotions (in ourselves or others) provide us with information and insight that is necessary for decision-making. David Eagleman[4] quotes an example of a woman with a brain injury, whose rational and emotional systems are disconnected. Consequently, she is unable to make choices between alternatives, such as which type of cheese to buy in a supermarket. There is too much information for her rational system to weigh up to make the choice, and because her emotional system is not effective she is unable to value one choice over another – she cannot make herself care about the choice. Decisions have both rational and emotional components. Think about how you vote – it is likely that some of your choice is based on your gut feeling.

At work, people choose (consciously or subconsciously) how much discretionary effort to exert, depending on how engaged they are with their manager, colleagues, work and the organisation. You can influence how engaged people are with you, how committed rather than merely compliant they are, by shifting your energy and communication to connect with them in a more emotionally intelligent way – being aware of your own emotions and managing them, as well as picking up on and engaging their emotions.

The EQ Equilibrium

When you communicate to engage people's emotions, they will feel more commitment and you will get better results for everyone.

Managing your own emotions and mood

Emotions and moods are infectious. The first step to being an engaging communicator is to be aware of your own emotions and able to manage them. This is a key part of emotional intelligence (the left-hand end of the EQ equilibrium). But it is often difficult to know what is going on in our own minds. Much of our behaviour is driven by unconscious processes – we do and say things based on automatic patterns without conscious thought. Even when we are aware of our thoughts and feelings, we often cannot explain *why* we are thinking or feeling that way. We may feel happy, but don't know why. We associate smiling with being happy but do we smile because we are happy, or are we happy because we are smiling? Which comes first, the emotion in the brain or the action in the body? People who work in call centres are advised to smile when they are on the telephone, even though the customer can't see them. It is believed that the emotion linked to physically smiling comes across in their tone of voice and enables them to take a more positive approach to the customer's problem.

When you are preparing to communicate, you can create a positive mood in yourself, which will help to create a positive emotional state in the people with whom you are communicating.

Here are three steps to managing your mood:

1. **See** yourself communicating successfully. To do this, picture yourself in the situation, observe yourself there, see what you are wearing and how you are standing or sitting. Then slowly think through what you are doing and saying, what you are thinking and feeling, what skills and qualities you have, what is important to you in the situation and finally what is your purpose in the communication. It can help to talk through this process with a friend or colleague.

   An alternative approach is to recall a time when you communicated successfully and again think through the same set of questions. What did you do and say, what were you thinking and feeling, what skills and qualities were you demonstrating – so that you can re-create the same positive mood when you need it. The figure below, taken from neuro-linguistic programming (NLP),[5] illustrates these steps.

Identity	WHO are you? What is your purpose?
Values and beliefs	WHY were you doing it? What was important to you about it?
Capabilities	HOW were you doing it? What skills and abilities did you show?
Behaviours	WHAT were you doing and saying? What were you thinking and feeling?
Environment	WHERE were you? WHEN was it?

2. **Hear** your own positive self-talk. It is really important to build up your confidence by reminding yourself of the positive aspects of what you are communicating. Our thoughts influence our emotions, which in turn influence how we act, and this affects the results we get. (You can remember this with the mnemonic TEAR).

Thoughts ⟶ **E**motions ⟶ **A**ctions ⟶ **R**esults

When we are nervous or worried about something, we tend to have automatic negative thoughts (ANTS) and these come out in our body as butterflies in the stomach, shaking hands and a trembling voice. This means we project our message less confidently and people pick up on our lack of confidence with the result that we less convincing. In most cases our negative thoughts are not logical, not realistic and certainly not helpful.

Before communicating, reframe these ANTS into positive thoughts so that you feel more upbeat and confident. This will come across in your voice and body language with the result that you will be more influential.

The table here shows an example of how to use the positive self-talk approach when preparing for a job interview – banish the ANTS in the left-hand column and focus on the positives in the right-hand column.

Potential negative thoughts	Positive self-talk
I haven't got the skills for this job	I've got skills in xyz
They've already decided who they want	I've got as good a chance as anyone
I've heard it's hard to get in there	I know other people who have got in there
There will be lots of competition	It's a popular job
Everyone else will have better experience	I've got relevant experience
They won't like me	I'm a likeable person
I'm going to be nervous	I'm going to enjoy it
I won't be able to answer the questions	I've prepared for lots of questions
I'll fail the tests	I've done tests before and no one gets it all right
I don't know what to wear	I'll ask what the dress code is

This trick of turning negatives into positives is a valuable technique for managing your emotions to create a more positive outlook. This in turn will enable you to perform better and have a positive impact on the people with whom you are communicating.

3. **Feel** the positive mood by reliving times when you have been in a confident, relaxed mood – recall how this felt and re-experience these feelings.

Mind and body are linked, so being aware of your body is an important aspect of managing your own emotions. The body tells the mind what mood we are in, and vice versa. If you manage your body and your energy to relax and behave 'as if' you are feeling positive, you will feel positive mentally.

Amy Cuddy,[6] a researcher at Harvard University, has classified different body positions as 'high power' or 'low power' poses. In general, the high-power poses are open and relaxed while the low-power poses are closed and guarded. The most well-known and versatile high-power pose is nicknamed 'The Wonder Woman' pose, in which you stand tall with your chest out and your hands on your hips. Cuddy advocates that we hold this pose for two minutes a day (in private) in order to start the day in a confident mental state. This may not work for everybody, but it is worth trying.

Being aware of what is going on in your body enables you to do something about it. When you are nervous you breathe with short shallow breaths, higher in the chest. One way to release the tension is to breathe more deeply in the abdomen. This is sometimes called belly-breathing and is often taught as part of mindfulness courses. Doing this breathing calms the nerves and puts you in a more resourceful state.

Think of a time when you felt relaxed and confident when communicating
What did you do and say? What did you think and feel?

Following these three steps (see, hear, feel) will enable you to be a more confident communicator and have a more influential impact.

Communicating emotions

We communicate emotion, whether we intend to or not, and people pick up on the emotions, whether we want them to or not. So, it makes sense to consider the emotions you want to transmit.

Try communicating different emotions through your tone of voice and body language.

Choose an emotion from the list below (the first six are the basic, universally recognised ones). Read any paragraph from this book to someone else, with the tone of voice and body language that matches the emotion you have chosen. Did they guess it correctly? What did you do with your voice and body language that communicated the emotion to them?

Emotion	What you did/said	What emotion they saw/heard
Anger		
Sadness		
Disgust		
Joy		

(Continued)

Surprise		
Fear		
Enthusiasm		
Calmness		
Reserve		
Organised		
Thoughtful		
Animated		
Patient		
Decisive		

Now choose another emotion from the list and this time, without speaking, carry out an action in the style of that emotion, such as carrying a glass of water and putting it down on a table. Can the observer correctly guess the emotion you are communicating? What did you do in your face, movement and posture that communicated that emotion to them?

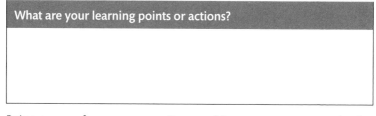

What are your learning points or actions?

Being aware of your own emotions and how you are communicating them affects whether your behaviour stimulates positive or negative reactions and emotions in your audience. Again, this is about ensuring that your impact on others matches your intention and that you create a positive emotional state in others.

Flexing your style to engage and inspire

The next sections cover how to flex your style according to the purpose you want to achieve, the style and situation of the person with whom you are interacting, and the stage of the communication process.

Flexing your style to the purpose

You can't change other people's behaviour – you can only change your own. But you can influence how other people behave by communicating in a style that engages the emotions to lead to the outcome you want. Think about how people feel when you communicate with them – put yourself in their shoes. How do you want them to feel? Bored, nervous, angry, confused? Or curious, confident, relaxed, clear? What do you need to do in the content and delivery of your message to elicit positive emotions? Managing your own mood (as outlined above) is the first step.

Choosing the best style for your purpose will help to generate positive emotions and responses in others. For example, in an emergency, you would probably take the mobiliser style – moving quickly, issuing instructions and exuding a sense of urgency. People would most likely respond by matching your pace and acting quickly. Similarly, when you want a deep discussion on a complex topic, adopting the synthesiser style – open, thoughtful, approachable – would create a consultative climate and elicit a more considered response from others. When you want to generate enthusiasm in others, an energiser style – persuasive, involving, expressive – would fit. And in order to create a controlled and measured response in others, a navigator style – calm, structured, sustained – might be the best choice. By shifting your own energy in this way, you will influence the emotions and mood of the people you are communicating with and this will help you to achieve the outcome you want and get their commitment.

When you adopt the movement and energy of another style, you will start to feel like that style and may experience the same inner drives. If you want to appear confident, harness the mobiliser energy – speak and move quickly, focus on moving towards the goal – and you will start to feel confident. If you want to appear approachable, harness the synthesiser energy – slow down and pause, look relaxed and friendly and listen to the other person.

Use the table in Chapter 3 (also Table 2 in the Appendix) to remind yourself of the physical and verbal characteristics of each style and try them out to communicate in a different style. Tips on specifically how to adapt your style to build rapport with each style are in Chapters 9–12.

Flexing your style to the person

As well as managing your own emotions, to be an engaging communicator you need to be aware of other people's emotions and be flexible in how you respond to them – the right-hand end of the EQ equilibrium. Here's a summary of the inner drives and stressors of each style:

	Drive	What to be aware of
NAVIGATOR	To plan how to reach the goal *'I need a course of action'*	They get stressed when they don't know what's likely to happen. Other people may feel they are inflexible.
MOBILISER	To get on quickly with the task *'I need action with results'*	They get stressed when nothing is being accomplished. Other people may feel rushed.
ENERGISER	To get everyone involved *'I need collaboration'*	They get stressed when they or others are not involved. Other people may feel it's chaotic.
SYNTHESISER	To consider all the options for achieving the task *'I need information to get the best result'*	They get stressed when they don't have enough input, time or credit. Other people may feel it's taking too long.

When you pick up cues that the person you are interacting with is in a particular style, you will have insight into what their needs are, and you can respond in a way that helps them get those needs met and avoid their stressors. See the tips in Chapters 9–12 on how to help people of each style meet their needs.

> A team of senior scientists in a large utility company needed to improve the engagement of their staff. We worked on how to develop their natural styles to become better communicators.
>
> All six people had responding (introversion) preferences, and there was a degree of groupthink and a tendency to dismiss other styles as wrong. Learning about the styles gave them a concrete awareness of their own impact on others, both positive and negative, and practical guidance on how to employ more outgoing, engaging styles to achieve better connections with their teams. One of the scientists realised that he had created a barrier to communication by positioning his desk such that he sat with his back to anyone who approached him. Moving his desk around was a quick win to be more approachable.
>
> They put together an action plan and implemented changes in how they interacted with their teams. This led to improved employee engagement scores in the subsequent employee opinion survey from 72% to 86%, at a time when the organisation's overall score went down, and they were delighted with this result.

Flexing your style to the person's situation

Sometimes it is helpful to adopt different styles and approaches depending on the circumstances of the person with whom you are communicating.

The 'Skill – Will' matrix is a useful tool to help you judge what style would be most effective to influence someone to action, depending on how committed (will) and how capable (skill) they are. This applies equally to colleagues at work as well as people at home.

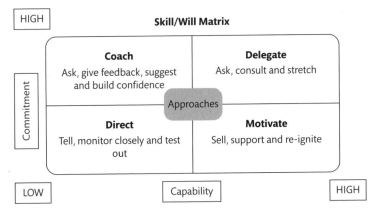

You can adopt different styles depending on where each person is:

- For someone low in commitment and capability, a directing approach might be appropriate, to clarify for them what to do and how to do it. In this case, a mobiliser or navigator style could be the most effective style.

- For someone low in commitment and high in capability, a motivating approach might be appropriate to help them become energised towards the task. In this case, energiser could be the most effective style.

- For someone high in commitment and low in capability, a coaching approach might be appropriate to help them work out and build their confidence in how to achieve the task. In this case, synthesiser could be the most effective style.

- For someone high in both commitment and capability, a delegating approach is likely to be most appropriate so that they can get on with the job in their own way.

For each style there are different strengths and pitfalls related to each approach. A mobiliser style will work well with someone low in commitment and capability who needs a directing approach. However, a mobiliser style can be a complete turn-off for someone who is motivated and would prefer to be coached to help them work out what to do for themselves, rather than be directed. If you have a synthesiser style, listening and being patient with your team member may come naturally to you and this fits well if a coaching approach is required, but this style may be ineffective, and could potentially be seen as soft by an individual who is not performing because they lack motivation.

The point is to be aware of when you need to flex your natural style and adopt the characteristics of another style, in order to adapt to the situation.

Consider your own style and identify your potential strengths and pitfalls for the different approaches you may need to take with people you want to influence. You may wish to refer back to the chapter about your own style.

Approach	Potential strengths	Potential pitfalls
Directing		
Coaching		
Motivating		
Delegating		

Flexing your style to the stage of the communication

At each stage of a communication, each style brings specific strengths and has particular pitfalls. Harnessing appropriate energies at each stage of a communication will enable you to be more influential, as follows:

- A strength of the Mobiliser may be to set goals at the beginning of a meeting, while a pitfall may be to cut off discussion of the topic before it has been fully explored.

- A strength of the Navigator may be to propose a course of action, while a pitfall may be to neglect to build rapport.

- For the Energiser, a strength may be to encourage the motivation to act, while a pitfall may be to be unrealistic about what can be achieved.

- A strength of the Synthesiser may be to bring in a lot of information, while a pitfall may be to delay decision-making.

The table below sets out what typically happens at each stage of a communication.

Consider where you believe your style brings strengths to the communication process and where there might be pitfalls for you and it might be more productive to adopt a different style.

Stage	Actions	Strengths you bring	Your potential pitfalls
Beginning	Build rapport Clarify purpose Set goals		
Explore topic	Find the facts Review the evidence Consider the bigger picture		
Evaluate options	Brainstorm options Discuss with others Be open-minded Ask questions Make proposals		
Make decisions	Set criteria for decision Evaluate options Make decision		
Agree actions	Set goals and targets Plan activities Evaluate risks and build in contingencies		
Motivate to act	Communicate decision and actions Monitor results		

What actions will you take to be a more engaging communicator?

Chapter 15

Power and charisma

When I left the dining room after sitting next to Gladstone, I thought he was the cleverest man in England. But when I sat next to Disraeli I left feeling that I was the cleverest woman.

Lady Randolph Spencer-Churchill

G oogle 'charismatic people' and the names that come up are people such as Barack Obama, Margaret Thatcher, Richard Branson and Oprah Winfrey. But you don't need to be a public figure to be charismatic – anyone can have charisma, even if they do not hold a formal position of power. Charisma is a quality possessed by some people that draws others to them, and it comes from their behaviour and their inner drives. Power often derives from a person's job or position and is the ability to influence how other people behave.

People with power and charisma are able to influence others, either because they have formal power over them, or because they have charisma which makes others want to follow them.

When someone has both power from their position *and* charisma, their influence on other people's behaviour can be enormous. Hitler had both position power and charisma, but lacked a moral compass and was able to inspire people to do terrible things. People with little formal power but with charisma are also able to change the course of events. Mahatma Gandhi and Nelson Mandela are prime examples of this. Some people are powerful but not charismatic. American presidents have enormous position power, though they may not have charisma (compare Bill Clinton or Barack Obama with George W Bush or Jimmy Carter).

In this chapter we will look at whether some styles are inherently more powerful than others and how people of each style can harness their natural talents to be charismatic. First, we will look at where power comes from.[1]

Sources of power

Power often derives from a person's job title or position, and this is known as 'legitimate' or 'position' power. Within organisations, the further up the hierarchy someone is, the more power they are likely to have over other people. Outside work, people may derive power from their roles, for example, as parents in a family or religious leaders within a community.

Having position power enables you to exercise two other forms of power – 'reward' power (carrots) and 'coercive' power (sticks). Parents exercise these types of power when they give gold stars or administer reprimands to their children. Managers in organisations may use incentives and sanctions in a similar way. Another source of power is being the gatekeeper for information or resources – hence the expression 'knowledge is power'.

There are two sources of power that come from the person themselves rather than from their position – 'expert' power and 'referent' power. Some people are acknowledged as the expert on certain topics and other people defer to their views. 'Referent' power derives from the personal qualities and the relationships that someone has. People with referent power are perceived as attractive, worthy and with a right to be respected. They are admired by others and this enables them to be influential. Referent power is essentially charisma.

Having power or charisma means that you can influence other people and events for good or ill, so there is also an ethical dimension to consider. The Milgram experiments[2] illustrate the impact of position power on other people's behaviour. The researchers found that many people obeyed instructions from people in authority to administer what they thought were severe electric shocks to others.

People who are motivated by their need for power may use their power with a positive intent for others – the 'socialised' power motive[3] – or only for their own gain – the 'personalised' power motive. In the latter case, people see power as an end in itself, as a personal privilege and they can be impulsive with little self-control or self-doubt, while people with the socialised power motive see power as a means to achieve desired goals for all. Interestingly, there seems to be a 'power paradox'[4] in which people who show empathy and enthusiasm and solve others' problems gain power, but once they have gained it, they seem to lose these qualities.

Power, or the lack of it, can also relate to class, race, and gender. These types of power are often exercised and experienced in subtle, sub-conscious ways. Reni Eddo-Lodge[5] believes that 'racism is woven into the fabric of our world' and researchers on gender equality have often talked about the 'glass ceiling'[6] preventing women from progressing.

Power and styles

Some styles seem to naturally appear more powerful than others. The mobiliser style, with underlying preferences for initiating communication and directing language, comes across as confident, decisive, and assertive. Their 'command and control' style and drive to get things done fits our stereotype of a leader. Where this personal style is complemented by other sources of power, such as position in the hierarchy, the mobiliser style can be a potent force – for good or ill. Donald Trump appears to have the mobiliser style, holds the most powerful position in the world and appears to have a strong personalised power motive. With this combination, he is likely to take a 'bull in a china shop' approach, push for quick action, and lack self-control and self-doubt. The 'Trump handshake' is one of the ways he uses his body language to exert power over others.

The synthesiser style does not immediately fit our stereotype of a leader, yet there are successful leaders with this style, including Barack Obama. People with the synthesiser style in positions of power can appear soft, as their style does not fit what people expect of a leader. This means that they have to find ways to speak with authority when necessary, for example, by initiating more communication and using a more directive or assertive style. Noam Chomsky explained the unpopularity of Jeremy Corbyn, prior to the 2017 UK general election, as attributable partly to his synthesiser style: 'he is quiet, reserved, serious, he's not a performer'.[7] During the election campaign, Corbyn overcame the downsides of his style to be assertive and confident in public appearances.

People with the energiser style take an initiating role in communication. Like Mobilisers, they tend to be out there, making contact and talking to others, so this gives them a starting point for having a powerful impact on others. People with the responding preference, the navigator and synthesiser styles, tend to be more internally focussed, they say less and often keep their thoughts and feelings to themselves. This means they will have less influence on others, so they have to make a conscious effort to communicate more, both verbally and non-verbally, in order to have a powerful impact. Theresa May's difficulty in communicating comfortably in public was probably a contributory factor to the poor results of the Conservative Party in the 2017 UK general election.

Preferences for using directing communication rather than informing communication also affect how power is perceived by others. People with the directing preference (mobiliser and navigator styles), who are comfortable telling people what to do, are often seen as one-up and more powerful than people with the informing preference (energiser and synthesiser styles), who prefer to ask and explain, and may be seen as one-down. This means that people with the latter styles may have to find ways to be more assertive in their choice of words, tone of voice and body language if they want to come across in a more powerful way.

Jiang had the mobiliser style and led a team of HR managers, most of whom had the energiser style. They all agreed that Jiang's strengths were giving structure, clarity and direction to achieve their goals. He was decisive and quick to get to the point. These characteristics, combined with the fact that he was the boss, meant that his team often felt there was no point in expressing disagreement or advocating other approaches. They did not feel engaged and involved (a key motivator for Energisers) and Jiang knew that they did not always speak up or provide him with the ideas and options he needed. By having an open discussion about their different styles, Jiang began to adapt his style to slow down, listen and encourage input from his team and they felt they had his permission to be more assertive in expressing their views.

When **Andy** learned about his synthesiser style at a workshop, he decided to 'say what I am thinking more often and simply, plus be more assertive and speak more confidently.' Two months later, he described the results of this changed behaviour. 'Others have accepted it when I have been directive. It has opened conversations that would not have happened otherwise. This has revealed additional information, but it also feels like the relationships have improved'.

The impression of power created by each style is complicated by gender. Women are typically seen as less powerful than men, and in some cases their style may contribute to this perception. There are probably more men with the directing mobiliser and navigator styles and more women with the informing energiser and synthesiser styles. This tends to fit our gender stereotypes of men as task-focused and women as people oriented. Energiser or synthesiser women have a double whammy to contend with – they are female *and* their styles are perceived as the one-down style. The energiser style fits our social norms about female behaviour – talkative and bringing people together – and in order to appear powerful, women with this style may need to hold back a little and be less chatty. Women with the synthesiser style may need to be more assertive and less accommodating in order to communicate an air of authority. Women with the mobiliser or navigator styles have the opposite problem and tend to be described as bossy, while a man with these styles is regarded as assertive.

Each style has a natural power base in its own core beliefs, drives and talents. Being true to your own style is a good foundation for having a powerful impact on others. But be aware of the need to draw on some of the behaviours of other styles to round out your own style. The table below shows the potential traps of each style and how to avoid them.

	NAVIGATOR	MOBILISER	ENERGISER	SYNTHESISER
Power base	Belief that it is worth the effort to think ahead to reach the goal	Belief that it is worth the risk to go ahead and act or decide	Belief that it is worth the energy to involve everyone and get them to want to...	Belief that it is worth the time to integrate and reconcile many inputs
	Focused energy	Determined energy	Engaging energy	Approachable energy
	Directive language	Directive language	Being a source of ideas	Being a source of knowledge and information
	Being decisive	Being decisive	Making others feel involved	Consulting others to get their input
	Measured, considered approach	Being out there and communicating	Being out there and communicating	Supportive approach
		Command and control approach	Enthusiastic approach	
Traps of this power base	Not communicating enough	Taking responsibility away from others	Overwhelming others with too many words and ideas	Accommodating others too much or ignoring their ideas
	Appearing inflexible	Appearing bossy	Appearing flustered	Appearing indecisive
Ideas for change	Share your thoughts	Step back and let others have a go – **emp**ower them	Say less and listen more	Clarify the process for decision-making
	Be willing to change your mind	Listen to others	Be decisive about where to focus efforts	Say what you think assertively

Charisma

Charisma is one type of power and comes from a combination of external behaviours (confident words, tone of voice and body language) with internal motivations (being authentic and passionate about your aims). Nikki Owen describes charisma as strong charm plus strong character.[8] Olivia Fox Cabane[9] says that people with charisma project presence, power and warmth through their verbal and non-verbal communication. The outcome is to make other people feel good, which in turn means they are willing to be influenced. Making other people feel good is a skill that can be learned and everyone can adapt their natural style to do this.

Charismatic people have:

- High self-esteem (covered in the next chapter)

- Ability to make others feel good

- Confident words, tone of voice and body language

- Passion and enthusiasm for their aims.

Making other people feel good

When we interact with others, we have basic social needs.[10] We want to feel good about ourselves and that we are:

- Significant – that we matter to others

- Competent – that we are respected

- Likeable – that others like us.

We have corresponding fears that can affect our behaviour:

- The fear of being excluded if we are not important to others.

- The fear of being humiliated if we fail.

- The fear of being rejected if others don't like us.

These are fundamental fears and the brain experiences them as acutely as if they were threats to our physical survival, and the flight or fight response can activate.[11] A charismatic person allays these fears by making people feel that they matter, they are worthy of respect and they are liked. So, you can develop charisma by behaving in ways that enable others to feel they are significant, competent and likeable, as well as maintaining your own self-esteem by believing the same of yourself.

If you don't have self-esteem, you will feel anxiety and self-doubt, which will prevent you from coming across confidently and with charisma. (See the next chapter for tips on how to build your self-esteem and self-confidence.) Bear in mind that behaviour is what you do, say, think and feel, so to come across with charisma, you need to do, say, think and feel the right things, not just about the other person, but also about yourself.

Holding healthy beliefs that we are significant, competent and likeable, and that the person we are communicating with is also significant, competent and likeable, is an essential starting point for communicating with charisma. If they don't matter to you, if you don't respect or like them, then this will affect how you behave towards them and the impact will not be charismatic.

Here are some tips on how to make other people feel good:

- **Making people feel significant:** Build rapport, show that they matter, listen, invite them to participate, include them, make eye contact, pay attention to them, don't interrupt them, make them feel special.

- **Making people feel competent:** Give praise, avoid criticism, don't make them feel they are wrong, ask their opinion, encourage them, don't mock them.

- **Making people feel likeable:** Express liking through your body posture, have an open and approachable manner, smile, soften your eyes, look friendly, express concern for their concerns, show empathy, ask them about themselves, feel goodwill towards them.

What can you do to make others feel good about themselves?

Many people find Barack Obama charismatic and he is skilled at making other people feel good. Brendan Cox, husband of the murdered British MP Jo Cox, was invited to meet Obama at the White House and wrote: 'He was warmer and even more approachable than I had hoped... he set us at ease...he charmed the kids.'[12]

Verbal and non-verbal communication

We all have the potential to be charismatic and make other people feel good. The table below shows some of the verbal and non-verbal behaviours of charismatic people.

Body language	Confident and centred posture
	Mirror body language to build rapport
	Eye contact with eyes relaxed
	Truly listen and show that you are listening
	Give reassurance (nodding, affirmation), but don't overdo this as it can appear subservient
	Show physical energy and presence
	Communicate positive emotions (see Chapter 14)
Voice	Lower the pitch (especially if you are female)
	Slow the tempo and introduce some pauses
	Drop intonation at the end of sentences
	Resonant voice
Words	Don't interrupt
	Don't make others feel wrong or bad
	Use assertive language – I think, I would like, I want
	Use 'and' not 'but' when disagreeing with someone
	Avoid saying 'You should' or 'You ought'
	Use open questions like 'What do you think?', 'How do you feel about that?'
	Know your subject and sound confident
	Show conviction
Inner drives	Know what you want to achieve (see Chapter 13)
	Check that you have a positive intention for others

Charisma and styles – harnessing your natural talents to be charismatic

Charisma, like your style, comes from external behaviour (verbal and non-verbal communication), linked to inner drives and positive intent.

Everyone has the capacity to develop charisma, by building on the power base of their own style and avoiding the traps. Charismatic people project power, presence and warmth and trigger positive emotions in others which make them feel good.

Here are some ideas for how to develop charisma for each style.

NAVIGATOR	MOBILISER	ENERGISER	SYNTHESISER
Show warmth	Be present	Slow down speech	Maintain eye contact when speaking
Initiate contact with others	Slow down speech and movement	Lower your tone of voice and add some pauses	Use assertive phrases
Smile	Make time for others	Reduce arm movements	Display expressive body language
Make eye contact when speaking and listening	Ask them what they think	Use fewer words – get to the point more quickly	Increase the volume of your voice and lower the tone
Soften the eyes	Listen actively and reflect back	Listen and let others speak	Avoid raising your tone at the end of sentences
Show interest in other people's personal lives	Relax your muscles and breathe deeply	Be more explicit about what you want to happen	Speak up more – think it then say it!
Give more explanation of your ideas	Control your sense of urgency	Focus on the topic and be specific	Use anecdotes and stories
Adopt an open posture	Practise mindfulness	Have a vision and a purpose you believe in	Don't give in to others against your better judgement

Note some charismatic behaviours to try out

Charisma can vary according to the situation. People can be charismatic in some circumstances and not in others and this is usually based on how much self-esteem and self-confidence they feel in each situation. The next chapter covers how to enhance and maintain your self-esteem so that you can communicate with confidence *and* charisma.

Chapter 16

Enhancing your self-confidence

If you hear a voice within you say 'you cannot paint', then by all means paint, and that voice will be silenced

Vincent van Gogh

Performers who are very charismatic on stage can appear very ordinary when you meet them in person. On stage their belief in what they are doing gives them confidence and they exude charisma, while off stage they have the same fears, uncertainties and doubts as the rest of us. We can't all be confident all of the time in every situation, but believing in our own ability and value helps us to feel more confident more often, and confidence leads to better performance. Football teams often get better results at home than away, because the support of the home crowd gives them confidence, and this boosts their performance.

Self-regard is a belief in your own ability and value. Believing that you are significant, competent and likeable makes you feel confident and able to communicate with others confidently. As we saw in the last chapter, you also need to believe that other people matter, and respect and like them. Otherwise, they will feel excluded, humiliated or rejected and will respond with flight or fight. The figure below illustrates these different positions and is known as the 'OK Corral'.[1]

HIGH		
	I'm OK, you're not OK	I'm OK, you're OK
	Critical or fight position	Healthy position
Self-regard		
	I'm not OK, you're not OK	I'm not OK, you're OK
LOW	Blocked potential position	Submissive or flight position

Regard for others HIGH

Ideally, we want to be in the top right-hand box, having a high regard for ourselves and others, so that we communicate with confidence and charisma. You will know you are in this position if you feel good about yourself and feel respect and liking for the people you are communicating with. You will want a win–win outcome and will behave in line with this aim, asking questions and listening to their point of view, as well as advocating your own.

If you believe you are ok but don't feel respect and liking for others (top left position), you will be critical, may compete to achieve what you want at their expense (a win–lose result) and your behaviour may make others feel bad rather than good. You will be in 'fight' mode and will push what you want without considering their point of view.

If you have low self-regard, and feel everyone else is better than you (bottom right position), then you will go along with what they want without articulating your needs. You will avoid explaining your position or inquiring about theirs and will be in 'flight' mode. This is a position of low self-regard and perhaps too high a regard for others.

Finally, if you do not feel good about yourself, nor esteem for others (bottom left position), then there will be little progress for anyone – a hopeless situation.

Here are some tips to develop self-regard:

- Don't put yourself down, known as 'self-discounting'. If you hear yourself saying negative things about yourself, you will believe them ('I'm no good at . . .', 'I'm always doing it wrong', 'Don't worry about me', 'It doesn't matter what I think', 'I'm always unlucky'). Instead, remind yourself of what you are good at and do some positive self-talk (see chapter 14):

    - 'Other people can do this, so I can too.' (I say this to myself on rollercoasters)

    - 'I'm a friendly person so people will like me.'

    - 'I'll make my own luck.'

    - 'I'm good at my job.'

    - 'My family love me.'

    - 'I've learned new skills before, so I can do it again.'

- Ignore put downs from other people: 'The trouble with you is you've got no sense of humour', 'Typical woman!'. Going along with comments like these chips away at your self-regard.

- Let compliments from others sink in. We often skip over them in embarrassment and brush it off by saying 'It was nothing' or 'Anyone would have done the same.' Instead, thank the giver of the compliment, reflect on it and notice the effect on you and how it makes you feel – hearing positive things about yourself builds your self-esteem.

- Share problems with others and ask for their support. It really is true that a problem shared is a problem halved.

- Give yourself some time every day to do something that is important to you. This makes you feel good and builds your confidence and self-esteem. Spending every day doing things you don't really want to do can make you resentful and put you into one of the 'Not OK' boxes.

And here are some tips to develop esteem in others:

- Make an effort to see things from other people's points of view – imagine what they might be thinking or feeling.

- Express your appreciation of other people. We often avoid giving praise to others through embarrassment or lack of skill, but giving people specific positive feedback is motivating and builds their confidence.

- Restrain your criticism of others – look for the positives first and remember that making other people feel good is more effective than making them feel bad.

- Avoid making others feel they have to defend themselves, so ask questions beginning with 'What' and 'How', rather than 'Why'.

- Take opportunities to connect with others. Invite friends for a coffee, drop by a colleague's desk and arrange to have lunch with a contact. This makes them feel valued and gives you the chance to get to know and genuinely appreciate them.

> *Lucy* and *Emma* *were both trainers and often found they were at loggerheads in meetings, rarely agreeing on a way forward. They were assigned to a project which meant staying away from home for a week. Neither of them was looking forward to having to spend time together.*
>
> *But during the week, over meals and while travelling, they got to know more about each other and their lives outside work, and started to appreciate each other as people. After the week away, they had greater respect for each other's views and were able to discuss their different perspectives constructively. They continued to meet for a chat from time to time and this helped them to get on better in work.*

Building your confidence

To get on well with others, you need to get on well with and value yourself. Behaving as though you do not believe in yourself, puts you into the 'You're ok, I'm not ok' box, and it can result in people losing their confidence in you and discounting your views, which can further under-mine your confidence. This section covers some strategies for building your confidence.

Behave as if you are confident

The mind and body are linked. What we think and feel affects our bodies and our external behaviour. When we feel confident, we stand taller, make eye contact and speak more assertively. People are more likely to pay attention to what we say. When we lack confidence, we stoop, shrink into ourselves and speak more tentatively. People are less likely to pay attention to what we say.

The converse of this is also true – our bodies and physical behaviour can affect what we think and feel. Behaving **as if** you are confident makes you feel confident. Here are some tips for behaving as if you are confident:

- Manage your body language: Breathe deeply to calm yourself, relax your jaw and your shoulders, stand tall, make eye contact, smile, look interested and focus on the other person rather than on yourself.

- Be aware of your voice: Slow down your speech, speak at a normal volume, not shouting or whispering and lower the pitch of your voice (especially if you are a woman).

- Talk positively to yourself: 'I am calm, it's ok to say what I want, I am safe.'

- Think before you speak: Pause to allow your rational brain to kick in rather than reacting to your flight or fight impulses. Plan what you want to say and how to say it.

- Use assertive language: 'I' statements such as 'I think, I'd like, I need' rather than aggressive language ('You should, you ought') or submissive language ('Don't mind me').

- Use 'and' instead of 'but' when disagreeing: 'I appreciate how you feel. And this is how I feel...'

- Prime yourself for a confident state of mind: Do something that cheers you up, write down three positive things that have happened at the end of every day and imagine yourself behaving confidently.

Create a good impression

First impressions matter. Creating a confident first impression will create momentum to carry you through an interaction. Here are some tips for small talk and networking:

- When you meet someone for the first time, repeat their name (so you remember it) and use their name when you speak to them as it makes them feel significant.

- Practise starting conversations in low-stress situations – with the postman, your neighbour, colleagues, a shop assistant – and note how they respond and how you felt afterwards.

- Think up questions to ask people, such as about their hobbies and interests, or holidays they are planning.

- Make a note of the names of their children and partner so you can refer to them next time you meet them.

- At a networking event, set yourself an achievable target (to talk to three people) and don't feel you have to work the whole room.

- If you are more extraverted, beware of being too loud or domineering.

- If you are more introverted, give yourself 'introversion breaks' by leaving a busy environment for a few minutes.

> *Jenn,* who had an initiating (extraverted) energiser style, used to get annoyed with her husband when they had friends around for meals or parties. He would often disappear into the kitchen and load the dishwasher while the party was in full swing. She felt he should be enjoying the party and chatting to their guests, as she was. He had a responding (introverted) navigator style and he eventually explained to her that the time in the kitchen was a welcome relief from talking and listening to others, and that it helped him to re-energise. Once she understood his need, she was able to relax when he disappeared and appreciate the work he did in the kitchen.

Consider how you might come across to others when you first meet them and consciously adapt your behaviour. Here are some of the traps (how you might be seen by others) and tips for each style:

	Traps	Tips
NAVIGATORS	Intense and serious	Make small talk and smile
MOBILISERS	Arrogant and impatient	Listen, ask instead of tell and slow down
ENERGISERS	Flustered and loud	Slow down, speak more quietly and listen
SYNTHESISERS	Quiet and boring	Speak more loudly and show energy

Set SMARTER goals and reward yourself

Having 'mastery'[2] experiences – setting goals and achieving them – gives us self-confidence.

You are probably familiar with the mnemonic SMART – goals should be specific, measurable, achievable, realistic and time-bound. Too often goals do not inspire us, they feel negative (losing weight or giving up smoking), too hard (increasing revenue by 10%, reducing costs by 20%) or just too big. Breaking big goals down into smaller goals and planning the detail of how to achieve them, taking into account all the things that can go wrong (the achievable and realistic parts of SMART), makes success more likely. Setting SMART**ER** goals – ones that are **e**xciting and **r**ewarded – is also more effective.

To make a goal exciting, it should be expressed in the positive (look slim, feel healthy), and ideally should be connected to a vision or a bigger purpose (be the best at customer service). Being able to imagine yourself in the future when the goal has been achieved is a powerful motivator, as is rewarding yourself as you achieve mini-goals along the way.

A common New Year's resolution, and one often broken, is to lose weight. This example demonstrates how setting SMARTER goals makes it more likely that it will be achieved:

- **S**pecific – to look and feel good wearing a smart outfit to my daughter's graduation.

- **M**easurable – fit into a size 12, be able to run up the stairs, get compliments from others and reach a target weight of 65kg.

- **A**chievable – do a daily 30-minute walk, find interesting recipes for salads and vegetables, eat salads at lunch time, eat protein and vegetables in the evening, use fruit for snacks when needed, drink water and walk up the stairs at work.

- **R**ealistic – if it's raining, do pilates at home instead of a walk, use different routes for the walk so I don't get bored, if I'm invited out for a meal, eat small portions (don't make it too hard).

- **T**ime-bound – graduation is in six months on 15 July, start on plan immediately and weigh myself every week to measure progress.

- **E**xciting – picture myself at the graduation looking good and feeling proud of my daughter.

- **R**ewarded – mark each milestone (a week when I walk every day, a week when I have tried three new recipes and a week when my weight has gone down) with something I like to do (a night out with friends or watching a film). The final reward is buying a new outfit for the graduation.

We often don't reward ourselves when we achieve our goals. Instead, we go straight on to the next big task, but there is evidence that rewarding ourselves gives us a sense of achievement and builds confidence. The reward does not need to be big or financial – just giving yourself a bit of time off to do something that you enjoy can be very motivating.

When you set goals, be specific on dates. Don't say the end of the month or the quarter, but the exact date, and put the dates in your diary, not just the date for the end goal to be achieved, but the dates for all the intermediate steps. Failing to plan means planning to fail.

Challenge limiting beliefs

Sometimes we hold beliefs that are unhelpful to us and undermine our confidence. Being able to recognise when they are getting in the way and acting as a brake on our progress, rather than helping and acting as an accelerator, is important for growing confidence.

A useful tool for challenging your thinking is a technique from cognitive behavioural therapy – the ABCDE[3] approach.

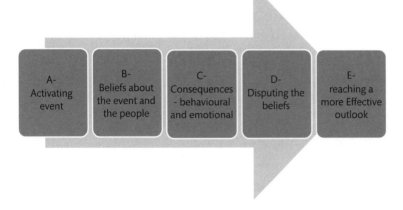

Here is an example of using this technique for a new employee who over-hears two colleagues discussing going out after work for a drink:

A Activating event – overhearing two colleagues talking about going out for a drink after work.

B Beliefs – she believes that it is wrong to leave people out of social events and that if someone is left out, it means they are not liked.

C Consequences – she feels upset that she hasn't been invited, decides that her new colleagues don't like her, and spends the rest of the day avoiding talking to them and generally feeling awkward in their company. This means that they don't get the chance to invite her along.

D Disputing the beliefs – there are other ways of interpreting their behaviour other than believing that they don't like her (they would have invited her later, maybe this was a long-standing arrangement).

Also, there may be other indications that she is liked (colleagues have taken her to lunch or offered to help her). Working though alternative explanations for the event brings the realisation that her belief that she is not liked is neither logical, nor realistic, nor helpful to her.

E Effective outlook – a more helpful outlook is to believe that there are many more likely explanations for her not being invited. If she accepts this, then there is nothing to hold her back from building a relationship with her new colleagues.

It is often our beliefs that lead us into misunderstandings with others and the beliefs can be so strong that they over-ride other evidence. However, it is possible to evolve a more constructive set of beliefs that enable a better outcome.

Moeen *had worked his way up in his organisation to a senior level. He believed that his success was due to getting on well with the directors and to being lucky. He felt they liked him and that this was why he had been promoted. He hadn't considered that the promotions were due to his own efforts and abilities. He was ambitious and wanted to get on further in the organisation, but his belief was holding him back – because he believed his promotions were due to being liked by the directors, rather than to his own abilities, he lacked confidence in himself and was afraid to assert himself when he needed to. He kept his views to himself, even when he believed the directors were making the wrong decisions and they felt he was not contributing at a senior level and therefore was not ready for promotion.*

During a coaching session, Moeen had a light bulb moment when he realised that being liked was a limiting belief and that being liked and progression are not the same. He worked out a more helpful belief, that being good at his job was related to progression and at the end of the session, said he felt like a weight had been lifted from his shoulders.

Think of a recent misunderstanding or conflict you have experienced and apply the ABCDE technique to achieve a more effective outlook.

Activating event	
Belief	
Consequences	
Disputing the beliefs	
Effective outlook	

Enjoy and do well

Having a clear picture of your strengths, knowing what you enjoy and how to deal with aspects of your role that you don't enjoy or are not good at (or both) enhances confidence. This tool is also useful when applying for jobs or evaluating your career direction. It can also be used for your roles outside work too.

	Enjoy	Don't enjoy
Do well	Strengths – plan to do more	Plan to reduce
Don't do well	Potential talents – plan to develop	Plan to fix

> *Jordan* *was struggling to cope with all his responsibilities and knew he needed to delegate more to his team of managers, but he couldn't decide what and how to delegate. He used this matrix to analyse what he really enjoyed about his work and how to deal with the parts he did not enjoy or was not so good at. This enabled him to put together a plan to develop his own skills in certain areas, and to identify what he could delegate to others. Delegating some activities meant that he had time to do the things that used his real strengths (in this case, financial analysis), which was a better result for the organisation as well as for him personally. Delegating appropriately also meant that his team got the opportunity to enhance their own skills and they took more responsibility for running the business and felt more confident. A win all round.*

Being able to spend time on the things we do well *and* enjoy is life-enhancing and gives us resilience when things go wrong. This is the subject of the next chapter.

Chapter 17

Building your resilience and re-energising

What matters in life: family first and foremost; work that fulfils; friends, beauty and fun

Robert Peston[1]

G etting on with other people is easier when we feel good about ourselves and about them, and when we feel positive emotions. But in life there are times when we face difficulties that lead to negative emotions – frustration, irritability, anxiety and depression. These emotions get in the way of us getting on with others. We all prefer to be with people who make us feel good, so even our friends may avoid us when we are struggling with problems. Resilience is the ability to bounce back from the challenges and setbacks that life throws at us and maintain a positive outlook.

This chapter is about some simple practices and techniques to help yourself to be resilient.

Pressure and symptoms of stress

We know that some pressure is good for performance. Too little pressure and we feel bored and demotivated, but too much and we feel stressed (Yerkes-Dodson law)[2]. Both situations can lead to physical and mental ill-health. The right amount of pressure is different for everyone – it's basically when the pressure is balanced by our ability to cope with it. Having the self-awareness to know when you are tipping beyond your point of equilibrium, together with the ability to manage your response to get back into balance, is crucial.

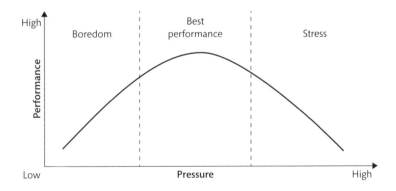

When pressure exceeds our ability to cope with it, we may experience some of the symptoms of stress.

Changes in behaviour	Physical symptoms	Mental symptoms	Emotional symptoms
Find it hard to sleep	Fast breathing	Be more indecisive	Get irritable or angry
Change your eating habits	Raised blood pressure	Find it hard to concentrate	Be anxious
Smoke or drink more	Tiredness	Suffer loss of memory	Feel numb
Avoid friends and family	Indigestion and nausea	Feel inadequate	Be hypersensitive
Have sexual problems	Headaches	Have low self-esteem	Feel drained and listless
Drive recklessly	Aching muscles	Lose self-confidence	Feel insecure
Develop nervous tics	Palpitations	Make rash decisions	Fear criticism
Show OCD behaviour	Panic attacks	Lose perspective	Feel hopeless
			Feel hostile

If stress continues in the long term, the physical and mental consequences can be very serious, so it is important to have ways of dealing with it. When asked how they deal with stress, people are more likely to name sedentary and solitary activities, such as watching TV, surfing the net, listening to music or reading a book, than active and group ones, even though more active strategies are proven to be more effective.[3] Active ways of dealing with stress are covered in the section on energising below.

How to manage the sources of stress

Generally, our options in dealing with sources of stress are the following:

- Control it – change the cause or source of the stress.

- Influence it – influence the source of the stress or change how we deal with it.

- Respond to it – use stress management techniques to reduce the impact.

In the figure below, the smallest circle at the centre represents the things we can control, the middle circle represents things we can influence, and the largest, outer circle represents things that happen that we can only respond to. For example, when I call a meeting, I can control the start and end times, and when I attend other people's meetings I may be able to influence the start and end times, but when my boss calls a meeting, it will start and finish when she wants it to. In the last case, there is no point in becoming stressed if the meeting overruns. I can't control the timings, but I can manage how I respond to minimise the stressful impact on me.

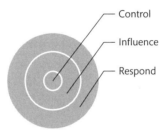

Categorising situations according to how much control we have over them enables us to choose an appropriate course of action. There is no point in becoming stressed about things we can neither control nor influence. However, sometimes we have more influence or control than we think.

Applying this model to the stressors of each style, we can see there are actions we can take at each of the three levels. At the centre are those things under our control when a potentially stressful situation arises. For example, we can take specific actions to ensure we fulfil our core drive. Someone with the navigator style, who is experiencing stress because there is no plan, can take control by proposing a course of action.

The middle ring is those things that we can influence. By changing our own reactions and behaviours, we can influence the situation and help ourselves. Someone with the mobiliser style, recognising they are feeling frustrated by an apparent lack of progress, may deliberately ease off their involvement. This can have the impact of allowing others to take control, which in turn starts to move things ahead.

The outer ring is those things which we cannot control or influence, so our only option is to choose our response. Someone with the mobiliser style, who is feeling frustrated by a lack of progress can deliberately take some time away from the situation to relax and calm down. If you are stuck in a traffic jam with no way out, the best response is to stay calm and use the opportunity to think or listen to the radio, rather than becoming angry and frustrated. Although we may not be able to change the thing that causes us stress, we can control our reactions to it, and by controlling our reactions, we may get a more positive outcome. Paul McGee[4] sums this up as follows:

The event + your response to it = the outcome

> **Veena** had a mobiliser style and managed teams planning customer installations. She was always in a hurry, moved and spoke fast, managed huge amounts of work, and rarely took a break during the day. She described herself as frustrated and impatient with the slow pace of others. She didn't delegate enough to her managers because she knew they wouldn't do it as well as she did. She put herself under pressure to get lots of things done, her style put others under pressure and her inner tensions also spilled over into her home life.
>
> She eventually realised that she could not control the pace of other people and that her own style had become an obstacle to her getting things done through others. By managing her own responses, by slowing down, taking a step back, letting others contribute in their own way, she started to get more collaboration in her team and her managers started to take more responsibility, which meant more work got done.

Think of a recent situation in which you felt stressed.

Where were you on the control/influence/respond map? What could you have done to take control or influence? How could you have responded differently?

Taking control and saying no

Taking too much on is a common source of stress for people. We sometimes agree to requests when a better course of action would be to take control and say no. Saying no is difficult for several reasons:

- We may feel it is selfish or rude to say no.

- We may feel guilty by refusing to help.

- We may not be skilled in how to say no.

- We may fear damaging the relationship with the other person.

However, the consequences of not saying no for yourself and the others involved are often worse than plucking up the courage to say no.

Here are some tips for saying no:

- Be aware of your first reaction to the request – if you have a sinking feeling, this is a good indication that you should probably refuse.

- If your reaction is more ambiguous, buy yourself some thinking time by saying 'I don't know, I need some more information', 'I need to think about it' or 'I have a few things on, I need a bit of time to weigh it up.'

- If you decide to say no, do so without excessive excuses or apologies by saying 'I don't want to...' 'I don't like...', 'It doesn't work for me...' or 'I can't do that.'

- Avoid explaining why the answer is no and avoid words that communicate uncertainty, such as maybe, perhaps and possibly.

- Take ownership of your decision and don't use others as an excuse.

- Acknowledge your feelings by saying 'I find this difficult', and theirs with 'I know you might be disappointed, but I can't help you this time.'

- Use a confident tone of voice and manner – speak calmly and slowly with a low pitch and make sure your voice goes down at the end of the sentence, so there is a sense of closure.

- Use confident body language – avoid fidgeting, maintain eye contact and stand tall.

- Once you have said no, don't hang around or look uncertain – say no and go, or move on to a different topic.

- A half-hearted yes when you really want to say no will find its way out somehow. You might make some pointed remarks or look resentful and the other person will notice this and feel let down.

- Remember that when you say no, you are refusing the request, not rejecting the person.

Asking for help

Asking for help is another way of taking control or having influence, rather than being a victim of other people's demands. We may believe that asking for help is a sign of weakness or failure, yet in most cases, other people are flattered when they are asked for help as it makes them feel significant and competent.

Here are some tips for asking for help:

- Decide what help you need and ask for it specifically and directly by saying 'I'd like you to bring the shopping in from the car please' or 'I'd like your help to finish the report please.'

- Make it easy to say yes and hard to say no. A request put negatively is easy to refuse, such as 'I don't suppose you could help me finish the washing up', while a request put positively is more difficult to refuse such as 'Could you help me to do the washing up please.'

- Deal with the other person's replies, but don't get side-tracked by red herrings – repeat your request.

Delegating to others

One of the hardest things for new managers to learn is how to delegate tasks to others. It is difficult to balance the need to delegate with the desire to retain control. But most people are motivated when they feel they have some autonomy over what they do and how they do it,[5] so it is important to delegate in such a way as to maximise their sense of empowerment.

Here are some tips for delegating:

- Decide on areas of responsibility to delegate (producing the monthly financial report) rather than one-off tasks ('Do the report today').

- Clarify your expectations with the person you are delegating a task to (the content of the report, when the final version is required).

- Delegate the responsibility with the appropriate authority to carry out the task.

- Ask open questions to ensure they understand and agree by asking 'What are your thoughts', 'How will this affect you', 'How will you go about it' or 'When can we review progress'.

- Agree with the person how you are going to monitor it – what progress reporting is required.

- Monitor progress on the due dates as agreed, not before.

- Ensure the person agrees to do it and has the skills to do it, and find out what help they might need from you or others.

- Use delegation as a way to give people the opportunity to learn and develop.

> **Samuel** had a mobiliser style and managed a car dealership. He got very frustrated when his staff did not action tasks that he gave them immediately. Although a specific task was a priority for him, they often had other more pressing tasks and customers to deal with first. He would check later in the day and become annoyed and critical when he found they had not carried out his request. They got more blame than praise and this was demoralising for them. Samuel was coached to agree specific dates and times for tasks to be completed, not check up on them before the due date and to control his impatience and urge to get things finished. Over time, his trust in his team grew, they felt more in control, and morale improved.

Finally, if you need to delegate a task that you would normally do yourself, such as attending a meeting in your place because you are too busy, then you are not delegating but asking for help. If you make this clear, people usually respond positively, otherwise they will feel you have just dumped extra work on them.

Responding to your sources of stress

Where we can't control or influence the thing that is causing us stress, then the final resort is to find positive ways to respond to it. Some techniques are similar to those for dealing with conflict, which is in itself often a cause of stress.

When in a stressful situation, the 'fight or flight' response kicks in and our emotions can take over our rational thoughts. So to avoid this try to:

- Take time out to control your reactions

- Move to a different location

- Use a quiet tone of voice and calm body language

- Be aware of and control your emotions – relax your body and breathe slowly.

These steps help to reduce the feelings of stress and put you in a more resourceful state to deal with the immediate problem.

For ongoing stress, the American Psychological Society, which researched resilience after the 9/11 tragedy, provides the following tips:

- Make connections.

- Avoid seeing crises as insurmountable problems.

- Accept that change is part of living.

- Move towards your goals.

- Take decisive actions.

- Look for opportunities for self-discovery.

- Nurture a positive view of yourself.

- Keep things in perspective.

- Maintain a hopeful outlook.

- Take care of yourself.

We can also improve our ability to cope with ongoing stress by building up our resources of energy. It is much easier to cope with challenges when we have physical, mental and emotional energy, but it is harder when we feel tired, drained and anxious. Having a plan to build up our resources is a key part of reducing the symptoms of stress.

Energy and re-energising

Put some SPICE in your life! When we talk about energy, we tend to think primarily of physical energy. But there are other types and sources of energy and giving attention to all of them builds resilience. A handy way to categorise energy is with the mnemonic SPICE:

- **S**piritual energy – this is what gives meaning and purpose to your life, why you get up in the morning, what is important to you and feeling connected to a higher goal beyond yourself.

- **P**hysical energy – this is the energy in your body, how physically active or energetic you feel.

- **I**ntellectual energy – this is your mind, how much your mind is engaged in what you are doing and stimulated by facts, ideas, thoughts and feelings, whether your mind is active.

- **C**areer energy – this is the energy connected with your work, whether you feel motivated and engaged at work. For many people, career energy can also be a source of spiritual and intellectual energy, by providing a sense of purpose and opportunity for using the mind (or the body, if you are an athlete).

- **E**motional energy – this is the energy that comes from relationships with family and friends, feeling valued by others, believing you are significant, competent and likeable and feeling self-worth.

Being able to manage these different types of energy is essential for building resilience. They are resources for resilience but they can become depleted if we don't take care of them. Spending too much time in one energy area is generally bad for us. Indeed, there is evidence that taking regular breaks from an activity helps to boost energy.[6] At work, taking a break from your desk, walking around, going to the coffee machine and popping outside for fresh air enable energy to be replenished and performance maintained. The same applies to students when studying, or to people at home. Spending too long on one task without a break depletes energy and enthusiasm for the task, while taking regular breaks is re-energising.

Just as energy levels fluctuate during the day, the same can be said of energy over longer periods of time, a week, a month, or even a year. At the end of a week at work, many people feel mentally and emotionally drained, and often sleep longer at weekends to recover. Accessing our other types of energy has a positive impact all round. Physical exercise, or reconnection with our sense of meaning and purpose outside work, is an important way to allow mental and emotional energy levels to recharge. People who suffer from seasonal affective depression (SAD) experience a variation of their energy levels between seasons.

For well-being and resilience we need a mix of energies. It's like having a balanced diet. The SPICE energy categories are like the carbs, protein, vegetables and vitamins that are part of a balanced diet. By accessing and taking care of a mix of our energies, we can build resilience.

Many of us spend a lot of time at work using the two forms of mental energy – intellectual and career energy. We don't access much of our physical energy during the day, so you would think that on leaving work we would be bursting with physical energy and keen to go for a run or to the gym. Surprisingly, we are more likely to slump in front of the TV, even though this is not helpful for relieving stress. Yet, if we do go out and access some of our physical energy resources, we feel invigorated, and after exercise we go home re-energised.

Focusing on one type of energy and neglecting the others can leave us feeling unbalanced and dissatisfied with our lives. The most common situation for people who work is to focus on career energy and neglect spiritual, physical and emotional energy needs. Sometimes our work fulfils our spiritual energy needs by providing us with a sense of purpose and meaning. But when we spend so much time on our work, we may neglect to spend quality time with family and friends and fail to access our emotional energy to give balance to our lives. At times, people fulfil their emotional needs at work by socialising with colleagues, developing friendships, and even having affairs. The consequence of not accessing and replenishing your emotional energy is that you start to lose your sense of being significant, competent and likeable outside work. Your sense of self-worth and your self-image come wholly from your work, not from your life outside work and this can lead to relationship problems at home.

People who work in roles that require emotional labour, such as carers, counsellors, nurses, social workers and mothers with small children often talk about feeling emotionally drained after using their emotional resources all day long. Their emotional energy becomes depleted and to let it recharge they need to switch their attention to some other form of energy. Having some intellectual stimulation or physical exercise can help them come back into balance.

Similarly, professional sports people use large amounts of physical energy (and emotional energy too when they are competing), and after their training or their match, they often choose mental activity as a way of recharging their physical energy. The tennis player Andy Murray spends time on his Playstation to relax – he is using mental energy while his body recovers.

Resources of spiritual energy can also be depleted. People who work in occupations where their focus is on working for the greater good can also feel overwhelmed, if they do not take some time to rebalance their energies.

Fortunately, there are ways to help yourself avoid falling into the low energy traps and instead take positive steps to build your energy and resilience.

Jamie knew that his work-life balance was poor. He usually got home from work after his children had gone to bed, he would eat with his partner, then spend an hour or more each evening doing emails, so they had very little time together as a couple. He was also aware that his lifestyle was becoming increasingly unhealthy – he rarely stopped for a lunch break, would take snacks on the run during the day, and took little exercise.

Learning about the SPICE energies helped him break down the problem and prioritise a few key things he could change: he decided to come home one night a week by 5pm, he decided to not do emails on weekday evenings, and he arranged a weekly cycle ride with a friend. These few simple actions made a big difference to how he felt about his life and his relationship with his partner improved.

Take the SPICE questionnaire, adapted from Harvard Business Review,[7] to assess how well you look after and manage your energy levels.

Tick the statements below which are true for you.	
Spiritual	
	I don't spend enough time at work doing what I do best and enjoy most
	There are significant gaps between what I say is most important to me and how I actually allocate my time and energy
	My decisions at work are more often influenced by external demands than by a strong, clear sense of my own purpose
	I don't invest enough time and energy in making a positive difference to others or to the world
Physical	
	I don't regularly get at least seven to eight hours sleep and I often wake up feeling tired
	I frequently skip breakfast or I settle for something that isn't nutritious
	I don't exercise enough – aerobic training three times a week and strength training once a week
	I don't take regular breaks during the day to truly renew and recharge or I often eat at my desk, if I eat at all
Intellectual	
	I rarely read a book, or visit a museum or gallery or take a walk in the countryside
	I spend much of my time reacting to immediate crises and demands rather than focusing on activities with longer-term value and greater worth
	I don't take enough time for reflection, strategising and creative thinking
	I work in the evenings or at weekends and I almost never take an email-free holiday

(Continued)

Career	
	I have difficulty focusing on one thing at a time, and I am easily distracted during the day, especially by email
	I don't have the time or resources to do my job as well as I would like to
	I spend too much time reacting to other people's demands and don't have enough control over how I do my job
	I feel my efforts at work don't achieve anything of lasting value or are not connected to the bigger picture
Emotional	
	I frequently find myself feeling irritable, impatient, or anxious at work, especially when work is demanding
	I don't have enough time with my family and loved ones, and when I'm with them, I'm not always really with them
	I have too little time for the activities I most deeply enjoy
	I don't stop frequently enough to express my appreciation to others or to savour my accomplishments and blessings

How is your overall energy?	What do you most need to work on?
Total number of statements ticked: ____	Number of ticks in each category: Spiritual ____ Career ____ Physical ____ Emotional ____ Intellectual ____
Guide to scores	**Guide to category scores**
0–4: excellent energy management skills	0: excellent energy management skills
5–8: reasonable energy management skills	1: strong energy management skills
9–12: just about managing energy levels	2: significant deficits
13–16: significant energy management deficits	3: poor energy management skills
17–20: a fully-fledged energy management crisis	4: a fully-fledged energy management crisis

Now think about what actions you could take in the five SPICE energy areas to look after them better. Here are some questions that can help you identify some actions.

- **Spiritual**: What are your top three values? How do you live them? What is important to you? How do you want to be remembered?

- **Physical**: How well do you look after your body? Do you sleep well, exercise regularly and eat healthily?

- **Intellectual**: How do you keep an active mind? What do you find mentally stimulating? What do you enjoy doing?

- **Career**: What do you want to achieve? Where do you get your plaudits?

- **Emotional**: How do you show appreciation to others? How and to whom do you express your feelings? What cheers you up when you feel negative?

Energy management action plan

Here are suggestions of possible actions to build energy. Pick a few that are relevant to you and write your own energy management action plan.

Type of energy	Ideas to build energy
SPIRITUAL	List your core values – how far are you living them?
	Make sure you do one thing that you find satisfying every day.
	Imagine five years from now – if things go really well, what things that you've done would make you proud and satisfied – what needs to happen now for these to come true?
	Find ways to do more of the things that make you feel good.
PHYSICAL	During your working day, incorporate breaks every 90 to 120 minutes.
	Manage your food intake to control the ups and downs in blood sugar level.
	Take regular exercise – choose the type of exercise you enjoy.
	Follow strategies to ensure you sleep well.
	Make a habit of taking a lunch break and getting outside.
	Learn to notice the physical signs of your energy flagging.

(Continued)

Type of energy	Ideas to build energy
INTELLECTUAL	Prioritise more effectively, watch the 'urgent but not important' habit.
	Set yourself goals on the added value tasks and break them down into manageable action plans.
	Put your important goals on your desk or desktop and do an action towards them every day.
	Reduce interruptions by carrying out high concentration tasks away from phones and email.
CAREER	Manage email better – disable email when you need to think, set up rules such as cc items go into a separate folder and only access email at specific times of day.
	Don't accept meeting requests unless you know the purpose of the meeting and why you are there.
	Block out time in your diary for the important tasks.
	Build in breaks between and after meetings.
	Each night, identify the most important task for the next day, and do it first.
EMOTIONAL	Create opportunities to spend time with people you like.
	Do things with friends and family.
	Reframe negative situations.
	Talk problems through with someone.
	Manage your physical state – practise relaxation and mindfulness techniques.
	Fuel positive emotions in others by making a habit of telling people what you appreciate about them.

Accessing your different energy resources and looking after them will build your resilience. Just as your body needs rest and sleep, so do the other types of energy – rest your mind, take a rest from your career, rest from striving for meaning and purpose and rest from emotional labour.

Connecting with the natural world by spending more time outside has been shown to have many benefits and positive outcomes for mental and emotional energy and in helping people deal with challenging times.[8]

> *When both my elderly parents were in hospital, I used a lot of emotional energy which was extremely draining. I was encouraged by others to give myself a bit of time off to play tennis (physical) and read a book (intellectual). This was good advice – giving myself a break and doing something different was welcome relief and helped me to re-energise so I was better able to manage the challenges of the situation.*

Responding and initiating preferences

Being aware of the balance of your attention between your inner and outer worlds is important when managing your energy – see Chapter 2. Everyone needs a mix of time with others and time alone, but the balance of this is different for each individual. Too much interaction can drain the energy of people who have a more internal focus of their attention, while too little interaction can drain the energy of people who have a more 'out there' focus for their attention. Be aware of where your balance lies, so that you can take this into account when you plan actions to maintain your SPICE energies.

Having good levels of energy across the SPICE categories will help you to channel your style energy positively to achieve good outcomes. However, when your resilience and energy levels are low, the energy of your style is more likely to be expressed negatively, leading to unwanted consequences.

Style	Energy on a good day	Energy on a bad day
NAVIGATOR	Focused	Tense
MOBILISER	Determined	Angry
ENERGISER	Engaging	Frantic
SYNTHESISER	Approachable	Anxious

By managing your SPICE energies, you will have a lot more good days than bad ones.

Resilience, energy and confidence are linked. By managing your resources of energy, you will be more resilient and feel more confident. This will enable you to make the most of your style, bringing your positive energy and personal charisma to your interactions with others.

As a final boost to your confidence, remind yourself of the talents you bring to interactions with others – and remember that we need the talents of all the styles to get the best results for everyone.

The table below has space for you to add some talents of your own.

Style	Potential talents
NAVIGATOR	Pushing for a course of action with focused energy Planning, monitoring, guiding and adjusting
MOBILISER	Pushing for action with results with determined energy Deciding, directing, mobilising and executing
ENERGISER	Pushing for involvement with engaging energy Persuading, energising, facilitating and brainstorming
SYNTHESISER	Pushing for the best result with approachable energy Defining, clarifying, supporting and integrating

A final few words

I've learned that people will forget what you said, people will forget what you did, but people will never forget how you made them feel

Maya Angelou

This is an exciting time in neuroscience. Our understanding of ourselves – our minds, brains and bodies – will continue to grow. Even so, there will still be misunderstandings and conflicts in families, between friends and colleagues, and with strangers. Interactions with people we don't know are made even more complex by the layers of difference added by class, culture, race, nationality and identity. Understanding the four styles and being willing to flex your style is a step on the path to self-discovery and closer connection with others. Using this knowledge, we can communicate with confidence and charisma to get on better with anyone and make a positive difference to those around us.

Appendix

Table 1 Key Behaviours Summary – *they tend to........*

NAVIGATOR Push for a course of action	MOBILISER Push for action with results	ENERGISER Push for involvement	SYNTHESISER Push for the best result
They tend to move in a deliberate way, speak with a measured tone and pace, and appear calm and focused	They tend to move briskly, speak quite quickly and appear straightforward and determined	They tend to move and speak quite quickly and expressively and appear enthusiastic and engaging	They tend to move and speak in an unassuming way, and appear patient and approachable
They create a course of action to achieve the desired result	They mobilise resources to get an achievable result	They engage others to get an embraced result	They gather information and input to get the best result
They make deliberate decisions, checking against a thought-through process	They make quick decisions with confidence	They make collaborative decisions to ensure buy-in	They make consultative decisions, integrating many sources of input and points of view
It tends to come naturally to them to plan, monitor, guide, adjust	It tends to come naturally to them to decide, direct, mobilise, execute	It tends to come naturally to them to persuade, energise, facilitate, brainstorm	It tends to come naturally to them to define, clarify, support, integrate

Table 1 continued

NAVIGATOR	MOBILISER	ENERGISER	SYNTHESISER
Push for a course of action	Push for action with results	Push for involvement	Push for the best result
They keep the group on track and help to anticipate problems	They lead the group to a goal and help to get things accomplished	They facilitate the group's process and help to raise commitment	They support the group's process and help to avoid mistakes
They may become stressed when they don't know what is likely to happen (or if a plan changes, until they get a new course of action), or if they don't see progress	They may become stressed when others do not share their urgency or nothing is being accomplished, or if they feel out of control	They may become stressed when they or others are not involved in what's going on, or if they don't feel accepted	They may become stressed when they don't have enough time or are not given credit for their efforts or if they are pressed to decide too quickly

Adapted from L Berens[1] and S Nash[2]

---

[1] Berens, L (2011) *Interaction Essentials: three keys to effective relationships in the workplace and beyond*

[2] Nash S (2011) *Contextual Coaching*

Table 2 Outer Appearance - *when in this style, you might demonstrate this behaviour*

	NAVIGATOR "What's the plan? Let's get it right"	MOBILISER "Let's get it done now!"	ENERGISER "Let's get started. Let's do it together"	SYNTHESISER "What result do we need?"
VOICE	Calm and measured tone Measured pace Pauses to think Silence feels natural	Straightforward and direct tone Fast paced Pausing feels like a long time Tends to fill a silence	Enthusiastic and animated tone Fast paced Pausing feels like a long time Tends to fill a silence	Gentle and patient tone Thoughtful pace Pauses to think Silence feels natural
BODY	Light-footed Puts things down carefully Moves in a deliberate way to the destination, making adjustments as needed Pressing and pointing gestures	Heavy-footed Puts things down heavily Moves quickly and directly to the destination Punching and flicking gestures	Heavy-footed Puts things down heavily Moves in a wavy line to destination, taking in people and information on the way Slashing and wringing gestures	Light-footed Puts things down quietly Moves in a wavy line to destination, taking in people and information on the way Floating and dabbing gestures

Table 2 continued

	NAVIGATOR "What's the plan? Let's get it right"	MOBILISER "Let's get it done now!"	ENERGISER "Let's get started. Let's do it together"	SYNTHESISER "What result do we need?"
TALKS ABOUT	The plan, who to involve and what to avoid Reasons and consequences	Results and actions to be taken Reasons and consequences	What's going on with people and who is involved Points of agreement	The outcome and information needed Points of agreement
MANNER	Formal and business-like	Straightforward and direct	Persuasive and enthusiastic	Unassuming and modest
ENERGY	Focused	Determined	Engaging	Approachable/open
APPEARS	Quiet, calm, intense and serious	Quick-moving, confident and decisive	Expressive, upbeat, casual	Quiet, laid back, friendly and patient

Adapted from L Berens[1] and S Nash[2]

[1] Berens, L (2011) *Interaction Essentials: three keys to effective relationships in the workplace and beyond*

[2] Nash S (2011) *Contextual Coaching*

Table 3 Inner Motivations – *when in this style, you might be driven by these factors*

	NAVIGATOR Push for a course of action	MOBILISER Push for action with results	ENERGISER Push for involvement	SYNTHESISER Push for the best result
AIM	To get a desired result	To get an achievable result	To get an embraced result	To get the best result possible
DRIVE	Pressing need to **anticipate** obstacles	Urgent need to **accomplish** actions	Urgent need to **involve** others	Pressing need to **integrate** input
CORE BELIEF	It's worth the **effort** to think ahead and reach the goal	It's worth the **risk** to go ahead and act or decide	It's worth the **energy** spent to involve everyone and get them to want to...	It's worth the **time** it takes to integrate and reconcile many inputs
DECISIONS	**Deliberate** and purposeful	**Quick** and expedient	**Collaborative** and engaged	**Consultative** and integrated
PRIORITY	To create a course of action to achieve the desired result	To mobilise resources to get an achievable result	To engage others to get an embraced result	To gather information and input to get the best result

Table 3 continued

	NAVIGATOR Push for a course of action	MOBILISER Push for action with results	ENERGISER Push for involvement	SYNTHESISER Push for the best result
POTENTIAL TALENTS	Planning, monitoring, guiding, adjusting	Deciding, directing, mobilising, executing	Persuading, energising, facilitating, brainstorming	Defining, clarifying, supporting, integrating
WANTS TO	Keep the group on track and help to anticipate problems	Lead the group to a goal and help to get things accomplished	Facilitate the group's process and help to raise commitment	Support the group's process and help to avoid mistakes
STRESSORS	Not knowing what is likely to happen Not seeing progress	Nothing being accomplished Feeling out of control	Not being involved in what's going on Feeling unliked or unaccepted	Not having enough input, time or credit Being pressed to decide before they are ready

Adapted from L Berens[1] and S Nash[2]

[1] Berens, L (2011) *Interaction Essentials: three keys to effective relationships in the workplace and beyond*

[2] Nash S (2011) *Contextual Coaching*

Table 4 Building your Emotional Intelligence – *Self Awareness*

If YOU are in this style...	NAVIGATOR	MOBILISER	ENERGISER	SYNTHESISER
You might come across as......	Too intense and serious	Too direct	Overly optimistic	Unassertive
	Slow to respond	Bossy and demanding	Lacking focus on the task	Going into too much depth
	Over-focused on details and process	Impatient	Too talkative	Taking too much time and meandering around the topic
	Not engaged with the team	Unaware of other people's feelings	Easily discouraged	Lacking clarity of direction
	Holding back and lacking enthusiasm	Unappreciative of other possible outcomes	Not mindful of the details or the need for structure and planning	Being slow to decide and to act
	Rigid by imposing structure and process	Alienating others by controlling resources	Frenetic by wanting to involve and enthuse others	Sub-servient by accommodating too many needs
	Not willing to consider all options	Not listening to team's ideas	Throwing in too many ideas	Making things too complicated

Table 4 continued

If YOU are in this style...	NAVIGATOR	MOBILISER	ENERGISER	SYNTHESISER
How you can help yourself.....	Practise speaking up at the right time	Recognise when you are frustrated	Moderate enthusiasm to be credible	Ask for time and space to work out your thoughts
	Use open body language to appear approachable	Use relaxation techniques eg deep breathing	Find someone to act as a sounding board so you can talk things out	Use more expressive body language when you have a point to make
	Be open to new ideas	Step back and give others time to think	Slow down and think things through	Be more assertive – speak more confidently
	Ask for time to think	Slow down and let them speak	Ask for input from others and listen to it	Summarise and make specific, pertinent points
	Write things down to help you clarify your thoughts	Consciously listen to them	Reframe negative reactions – put them in perspective	Find ways to get heard in a group and to be listened to without being interrupted
	Plan how to disclose your thoughts appropriately rather than saying nothing	Avoid being critical of them and their ideas	Give direction rather than information ie be explicit about what you want	Give direction rather than information ie be explicit about what you want
	Give information rather than direction ie show you are open to other ideas	Build in time delays to think before you act	Use techniques to restore your self-belief eg positive mental thinking	Reward yourself when you achieve something that's important to you
	Make sure you are able to get away and have time to yourself	Give information rather than direction ie don't make all the decisions		
		Review your work/life balance		

Table 5 Building your Emotional Intelligence – *Awareness of Others*

IF THEY are this style...	NAVIGATOR	MOBILISER	ENERGISER	SYNTHESISER
Remember that they ...	Show **focused** energy	Show **determined** energy	Show **engaging** energy	Show **approachable** energy
	Aim to get a **desired** result	Aim to get an **achievable** result	Aim to get an **embraced** result	Aim to get the **best result**
	Are driven by a pressing need to **anticipate** obstacles	Are driven by an urgent need to **accomplish** actions	Are driven by an urgent need to **involve** others and be involved	Are driven by a pressing need to **integrate** input
	Believe it is worth the **effort** to think ahead and reach the goal	Believe it's worth the **risk** to go ahead and act or decide	Believe it is worth the **energy** to involve everyone and get them to want to...	Believe it's worth the **time** it takes to integrate and reconcile many inputs
	Make **deliberate** decisions	Want **quick** decisions	Want **collaborative** decisions	Want **consultative** decisions
	May be stressed when they don't know what is likely to happen	May be stressed when nothing is being accomplished	May be stressed when they are not involved in what's going on	May be stressed when they don't have enough input, time or credit

Table 5 continued

If THEY are this style...	NAVIGATOR	MOBILISER	ENERGISER	SYNTHESISER
How to shift towards them...	Be calm, direct, matter of fact	Be clear and concise – get to the point quickly	Start with small talk	Be open and friendly but not too expressive
	Slow down, pause and listen, with intermittent eye contact	Use a fast pace, strong tone of voice and direct eye contact	Use a fast pace, be animated, and expressive in body language	Make eye contact and use a softer voice, be more "low key"
	Stay focused, don't get side-tracked	Show you appreciate the urgency	Listen as they talk things through and show interest	Allow pauses for thinking time
	Be patient as they express their thoughts	Do small talk only when the main issue has been addressed	Appear open and show enthusiasm	Listen to them without interruption
	Don't invade their space	Tell them what you are doing and by when	Reinforce ideas with positive comments	Ask questions and listen carefully to the answers
	Limit small talk	Don't talk too much	Give information in an upbeat tone of voice	Give them time to reflect and integrate
	Let them know of changes to the plan	Help them to slow down, stand back and observe	Use personal examples	Ask them where they are in their thoughts
	Emphasise key milestones	Tell them the reasons for things	Highlight the benefits of some options	Don't pressure them to make a decision immediately
	Talk about the goal and movement towards it	Give them specifics	Put a positive spin on your ideas	Offer choices and pros and cons
	Encourage them to disclose their thinking and details	Push back if necessary, they don't mind	Act as a sounding board for them to help them think things through	Give them credit for their input
	Think things through – don't jump in	Join them in their humour		

Endnotes

Acknowledgements and Setting the Scene

1) Jung, C G (1923) *Psychological Types*

2) Keirsey, D and Bates, M (1978) *Please Understand Me: Character and Temperament Types*

3) Merrill, D W and Reid, R H (1991) *Personal Styles and Effective Performance*

4) Bolton, R and Bolton, D G (2009) *People Styles at Work....and Beyond*

5) Marston, W M (1928) *Emotions of Normal People*

6) Geier, J and Downey, D (1989) *Energetics of Personality, Personality Analysis*

7) Vaillant, G, (2012) *Triumphs of Experience: The Men of the Harvard Grant Study*

8) Berens, L (2011) *Interaction Essentials: Three keys to effective relationships in the workplace and beyond*

Chapter 1

1) Burkeman, O from an article in *The Guardian* newspaper 7 January 2016

2) Berens, L *Understanding yourself and others: An Introduction to Interaction Styles 2.0*

3) Goleman, D (1996) *Emotional Intelligence: Why it can matter more than IQ*

4) Gardner, H (1983) *Frames of Mind*

5) Ekman, P (1992) 'Facial expression of emotion – new findings, new questions', *Psychological Science*

6) Salovey, P and Mayer, J D (1990) 'Emotional Intelligence', *Imagination, Cognition and Personality*

7) Goleman, Boyatzis and McKee (2013) *Primal Leadership: Unleashing the Power of Emotional Intelligence*

8) De Waal, F (2009) *The Age of Empathy; Nature's Lessons for a Kinder Society*

9) Newman, M (2014) *Emotional Capitalists: The Ultimate Guide to Developing Emotional Intelligence for Leaders*

10) Uwe Krueger on BBC Radio 4 'In the Balance – EI and Business', January 2014

11) Sigal Barsade, Professor of Management, Wharton School, University of Pennsylvania on BBC Radio 4 as above

12) Mlodinow, L (2012) *Subliminal: The New Unconscious and what it teaches us*

13) Eagleman, D (2015) *The Brain: The Story of You*

14) Mlodinow, L (2012) *Subliminal: The New Unconscious and what it teaches us*

15) Adelson, E, Professor of Vision Science at MIT, 1995

16) McGurk, H and MacDonald, J (1976) 'Hearing Lips and Seeing Voices', *Nature 264*

17) Berger, J (2016) *Invisible Influence: the hidden forces that shape behaviour*

18) Loftus, E (1999) 'Lost in the mall: Misrepresentations and misunderstandings', *Ethics & Behavior*

19) Mlodinow, L (2012) *Subliminal: The New Unconscious and what it teaches us*

20) Eagleman, D (2015) *The Brain: The Story of You*

21) Mlodinow, L (2012) *Subliminal: The New Unconscious and what it teaches us*, p 104

22) Peters, S *The Inner Chimp*

23) Mehrabian, A (1981) *Silent Messages: Implicit Communication of Emotions and Attitudes*

24) Epley, N (2014) *Mindwise: How we understand what others think, believe, feel and want*

25) Mlodinow, L (2012) *Subliminal: The New Unconscious and what it teaches us*

26) Self, R (ed) (2005) *The Neville Chamberlain Diary Letters: The Downing Street Years*

27) Cook, M (1998) *Personnel Selection: Adding Value through People*

28) Epley, N (2014) *Mindwise: How we understand what others think, believe, feel and want*, p 31

29) Vanderbilt, T (2016) *You May Also Like: Taste in an Age of Endless Choice*

30) Maddocks, J (2014) *Emotional Intelligence at Work – how to make change stick*

Chapter 2

1) Nash, S (2011) *Contextual Coaching*

2) Costa, P and McCrae, R (1985) *The NEO Personality Inventory Manual*

3) Cain, S (2012) *Quiet: The Power of Introverts in a World that Can't Stop Talking*

4) Kendall, E (1998) *Myers Briggs Type Indicator: European English Edition*

Chapter 3

1) Marston, W M (1928) *Emotions of Normal People*

2) Berens, L (2011) *Interaction Essentials: Three keys to effective relationships in the workplace and beyond*

3) Nash, S (2011) *Contextual Coaching*

4) Cole, A www.cole-face.co.uk

Chapter 4

1) Thomas Kilmann conflict inventory

Chapter 5

1) Thomas Kilmann conflict inventory

Chapter 6

1) Thomas Kilmann conflict inventory

Chapter 7

1) Thomas Kilmann conflict inventory

Chapter 8

1) Newman, M (2014) *Emotional Capitalists: The Ultimate Guide to Developing Emotional Intelligence for Leaders*

2) Heinrichs, J (2013) *Thank you for Arguing: What Aristotle, Lincoln, and Homer Simpson can teach us about the Art of Persuasion*

Chapter 13

1) Mehrabian, A (1981) *Silent messages: Implicit communication of emotions and attitudes*

2) O'Connor, J and Seymour, J (1990) *Introducing NLP: Psychological Skills for Understanding and Influencing People*

3) Powell, J (1999) *Why am I afraid to tell you who I am?*

4) Galbraith, J K (1971) *Economics, Peace and Laughter*

5) Senge, P (1994) *The Fifth Discipline Fieldbook*

Chapter 14

1) Goleman, D, Boyatzis, R and McKee, A (2004) *Primal Leadership*

2) Corporate Leadership Council

3) Sigal Barsade, Prof of Management, Wharton School, University of Pennsylvania on BBC Radio 4 'In the Balance – EI and Business', January 2014

4) Eagleman, D (2015) *The Brain: the Story of You*

5) O'Connor, J and Seymour, J (1990) *Introducing NLP*

6) Cuddy, A (2015) *Presence: Bringing Your Boldest Self to Your Biggest Challenges*

Chapter 15

1) French, J and Raven, B (1959) *The Bases of Power*

2) Milgram, S (1963) 'Behavioral Study of Obedience' *Journal of Abnormal and Social Psychology 67*

3) McClelland, D and Burnham, D (1976) 'Power is the great motivator' *Harvard Business Review*

4) Keltner, D (2016) *The Power Paradox: how we gain and lose influence*

5) Eddo-Lodge, R (2017) *Why I'm No Longer Talking to White People about Race*

6) Hymowitz, C and Schellhardt, T (1986) 'The Glass Ceiling: Why Women Can't Seem to Break the Invisible Barrier that Blocks them from the Top Jobs', *Wall Street Journal*

7) Noam Chomsky quoted in *The Guardian* newspaper, 11 May 2017

8) Owen, N (2015) *Charismatic to the Core: a fresh approach to authentic leadership*

9) Fox Cabane, Olivia (2012) *The Charisma Myth: master the art of personal magnetism*

10) Schutz, W (1958) *FIRO: a three-dimensional theory of interpersonal behaviour*

11) Burnett, D (2016) *The Idiot Brain: a neuroscientist explains what your head is really up to*

12) Cox, B (2017) *Jo Cox: more in common*

Chapter 16

1) Ernst, F (1971) The OK Corral: the grid for get-on-with in *Transactional Analysis Journal*

2) Pink, D (2009) Drive: *The surprising truth about what motivates us*

3) Neenan, M and Dryden, W (2002) *Life Coaching: A Cognitive Behavioural Approach*

Chapter 17

1) Peston, Robert, BBC's Economics editor writing in 2013 in *The Telegraph* about his wife's death from cancer

2) Yerkes, R M, Dodson, J D (1908). *'The relation of strength of stimulus to rapidity of habit-formation'*. Journal of Comparative Neurology and Psychology.

3) Hackston, J and Moyle, P (2013) *Stress doesn't have to be distressing: understanding stress and building resilience*

4) McGee, P (2011) *S.U.M.O. The Straight-talking Guide to Succeeding in Life*

5) Pink, D (2011) *Drive: the surprising truth about what motivates us*

6) Kleitman, N, *'Basic rest-activity cycle—22 years later'*, Journal of Sleep Research & Sleep Medicine, Vol 5(4), Dec 1982, pp 311–17

7) Schwartz, T and McCarthy, C, *'Manage your Energy not your Time'*, Harvard Business Review, October 2007

8) Friedman, L F and Loria, K (2016) '11 Scientific Reasons you should be spending more time outside', *Business Insider UK*

Index